EXLIBRIS

CHRISTMAS
SONGS
and
THEIR STORIES

Books by Herbert H. Wernecke
Published by The Westminster Press

CHRISTMAS SONGS AND THEIR STORIES
THE BOOK OF REVELATION SPEAKS TO US

CHRISTMAS SONGS

SONGS

and

THEIR STORIES

by Herbert H. Wernecke

Philadelphia
THE WESTMINSTER PRESS

Contents

INTRODUCTION

The songs in this collection were selected on the basis that the songs are well known and are commonly used. Their stories have been brought together in response to requests that indicate keen interest in and a real need for them.

The word "song" is used in the title of the book rather than "carol" or "hymn" because the line of demarcation is not clear today; even in the time of Augustine it was in dispute. "Carols" are supposed to have originated from circle dances (New Year, Easter, springtime, harvest, as well as Christmas), the older ones, like folk songs, having come directly from the hearts of the people, so that the authors of both words and music have often been forgotten. "Hymns," on the other hand, are religious poems of a lyrical character.

While the carol narrates the story of the star, the shepherds, and the Wise Men or some other aspect of the Christmas observance in a festive or playful manner, the hymn is essentially devotional, singing the praise of God. In France, all songs pertaining to the Christmas season, whether hymns or carols, are called "noëls." In England the same word, but spelled "nowel," is similarly used.

For convenience in study and reference, the familiar words are printed for the Christmas songs here discussed. Music for these songs can be found in standard hymnals and carol collections.

1 *All My Heart This Night Rejoices*

Paul Gerhardt, 1653   Ebeling (Bonn)
Tr. by Catherine Winkworth, 1858   Johann Georg Ebeling, 1666

All my heart this night rejoices,
    As I hear,
    Far and near,
Sweetest angel voices;
" Christ is born," the choirs are singing,
    Till the air,
    Everywhere,
Now with joy is ringing.

Hark! a voice from yonder manger,
    Soft and sweet,
    Doth entreat,
" Flee from woe and danger;
Brethren, come; from all that grieves you
    You are freed;
    All you need
I will surely give you."

Come, then, let us hasten yonder;
    Here let all,
    Great and small,
Kneel in awe and wonder,
Love Him who with love is yearning;
    Hail the Star
    That from far
Bright with hope is burning.

Paul Gerhardt, author of this hymn, ranks with Martin Luther as one of the greatest of German hymn writers. Some authorities call him the most beloved, since in most hymnbooks he outranks Luther four to one, no doubt because of his less belligerent tone and more experiential emphasis.

He was born in 1607 in Graefenhainichen, near Wittenberg, son of the burgomaster (mayor). He studied at Wittenberg, but hope and opportunity were deferred by war (the Thirty Years' War) and poverty. After serving as a tutor in Berlin, he was ordained to the ministry in 1651, at the age of forty-four, and then spent six years at a church in Mittenwalde, where he also began to publish his hymns. His fame led to his becoming pastor of the Church of St. Nicholas in Berlin. Though eminently successful, he was ejected from the church by Elector Frederick William, who forbade free discussion of the differences between the Lutheran and the Reformed Churches. Following the death of his wife and four of his children, he went with the one remaining child to a small parish in Luebben, continuing his preaching and hymn writing until his death, June 7, 1676.

The hymn before us is dated 1653, just at the time when the author was in the midst of severe personal suffering. Except for the call in stanza two to " come; from all that grieves you You are freed," one could never surmise this, for the song is characterized by a dominant triumphant note, the product of a deep, trusting faith. After this beautiful song appeared in Johann Crüger's *Praxis Pietatis Melica,* in Berlin, it was widely used in its native land.

This carol-hymn has been described as " a glorious series of Christmas thoughts laid as a garland on the manger of Bethlehem." Christmas night in Bethlehem is pictured, the angel choir, and an imagined invitation from the Babe in the manger. Its carol-like quality is indicated by the fact that just the reading of the verses sets one's heart to singing, partly due, no doubt, to the quaint trochaic meter, a favorite among Germans for many generations and lately becoming increasingly popular in America.

Gerhardt's original fifteen stanzas were reduced to ten in Miss Winkworth's translation in her *Lyra Germanica,* 1858, and most hymnals now use three. While several tunes have been used with this hymn, it is most commonly sung with " Ebeling," or " Bonn," composed in 1666 by Johann Georg Ebeling (1637–1676), cantor of St. Nicholas Church in Berlin and director of music in a college of the same name.

While this tune does not have the swing of "Stella," written by the noted Horatio Parker in 1893, it is closer to its folk-song, carol-like character. It should be sung joyously but reverently so that the mystical significance of the words may come to full expression.

---

2   *Angels, from the Realms of Glory*

James Montgomery, 1816

Regent Square
Henry Smart, 1867

Angels, from the realms of glory
    Wing your flight o'er all the earth;
Ye who sang creation's story,
    Now proclaim Messiah's birth:
Come and worship, come and worship,
Worship Christ, the newborn King.

Shepherds in the fields abiding,
    Watching o'er your flocks by night,
God with man is now residing,
    Yonder shines the infant Light:
Come and worship, come and worship,
Worship Christ, the newborn King.

Sages, leave your contemplations,
    Brighter visions beam afar;
Seek the great Desire of nations,
    Ye have seen His natal star:
Come and worship, come and worship,
Worship Christ, the newborn King.

Saints before the altar bending,
    Watching long in hope and fear,
Suddenly the Lord, descending,
    In His temple shall appear:
Come and worship, come and worship,
Worship Christ, the newborn King.

James Montgomery (1771–1854), greatest of the Moravian hymn writers, was the author of over four hundred hymns. Belonging to a devout peasant family in Ayrshire, Scotland, he entered the Moravian School at Fulneck, near Leeds, England, to study for the ministry. His greater interest in writing poetry caused him to leave school, and after several irregular jobs, he became editor of *The Sheffield Iris,* a liberal journal. Though twice imprisoned for his liberal utterances, he devoted himself the more diligently to his literary work, with such excellent results that of his four hundred hymns one hundred are still in use. Hence he ranks with Wesley and Watts in this field. He himself said that each hymn had been born of a distinct Christian experience.

Even as all his hymns show a wide knowledge of Scripture, we find in these four stanzas a series of pictures from the Nativity stories — the angels, the shepherds, the Wise Men, and the saints, who, like Simeon and Anna, were waiting for the consolation of Israel.

The fourth stanza refers to Mal. 3:1, "The Lord, whom ye seek, shall suddenly come to his temple, even the messenger of the covenant, whom ye delight in: behold, he shall come, saith the Lord of hosts." Possibly the theme of the entire song also reflects Job 38:7, "The morning stars sang together, and all the sons of God shouted for joy."

One writer says of this hymn, "For comprehensiveness, appropriateness of expression, force and elevation of sentiment, it may challenge comparison with any hymn that was ever written, in any language or country."

The composer, Henry Smart (1813–1879), turned from the legal profession to devote his life to music. The inspiring melody for this hymn was composed in 1867 when the composer was blind, and therefore it had to be committed to paper through dictation. The tune received its name, " Regent Square," from the most prominent Presbyterian church in London of that day.

---

3 Angels We Have Heard on High

Traditional Carol   French-English Carol Melody

Angels we have heard on high,
  Sweetly singing o'er the plains,
And the mountains in reply
  Echoing their joyous strains.
    Gloria in excelsis Deo!
    Gloria in excelsis Deo!

Shepherds, why this jubilee?
  Why your joyous strains prolong?
What the gladsome tidings be
  Which inspire your heavenly song?

Come to Bethlehem, and see
  Him whose birth the angels sing;
Come, adore on bended knee
  Christ the Lord, the newborn King.

See Him in a manger laid
  Whom the choirs of angels praise;
Mary, Joseph, lend your aid,
  While our hearts in love we raise.

(Music available in *Noëls,* H. T. FitzSimons Company, Chicago, Ill.; *The Christmas Carolers' Book; The Hymnal,* Evangelical and Reformed Church, 1941.)

G loria in excelsis Deo " (glory to God in the highest) is the Latin version of what the angels sang on the night of the Nativity. The words as we have them in the song are traditional.

There is a tradition that Pope Telesphorus, whose pontificate is placed at about 125–136, ordained that all should sing the " Gloria in Excelsis Deo " on Christmas: " On the birthday of the Lord, Masses should be said at night . . . and the angelic hymn ' Gloria in Excelsis Deo ' should be said before the sacrifice." Others claim that the custom did not originate until the third century at the very earliest.

The tune is an arrangement of a French carol melody, whereas the choral refrain may have been taken from a Latin chorale of the late medieval period.

Because it was sung first in England by the Westminster Abbey Choir, or because it has frequently been sung there in the Christmas season, it is at times called the " Westminster Carol."

The melody is impressive in its simplicity. The joyousness of the rhythm brings to mind children's voices, clear and melodious, a genuine echo of the angelic choir on that starry night on the plains of Judea.

---

4 *As with Gladness Men of Old*

Wm. C. Dix, 1860

Dix
Conrad Kocher, 1838

As with gladness men of old
Did the guiding star behold;
As with joy they hailed its light,
Leading onward, beaming bright;
So, most gracious God, may we
Evermore be led to Thee.

As with joyful steps they sped
To that lowly manger bed,

There to bend the knee before
Him whom heaven and earth adore;
So may we with willing feet
Ever seek the mercy seat.

As they offered gifts most rare
At that manger rude and bare,
So may we with holy joy,
Pure and free from sin's alloy,
All our costliest treasures bring,
Christ, to Thee, our heavenly King.

Holy Jesus, every day
Keep us in the narrow way;
And, when earthly things are past,
Bring our ransomed souls at last
Where they need no star to guide,
Where no clouds Thy glory hide.

In the heavenly country bright
Need they no created light;
Thou its Light, its Joy, its Crown,
Thou its Sun which goes not down;
There forever may we sing
Hallelujah to our King!

This Epiphany or Christmas carol was written by William C. Dix 1837–1898) when he was twenty-three years of age. He relates that while he was recovering from an illness, he read the gospel for that day (Epiphany festival, Matt. 2:1-12) and before evening had completed these immortal verses. It is, therefore, a song in the night, a longing for more light and joy and power. The son of a surgeon, he was trained to be a merchant and moved to Glasgow in 1863 to take an important position in a marine insurance office. Among some forty hymns we owe to him, this one, along with "Come Unto Me, Ye Weary," is found in nearly all hymn collections in English-speaking countries.

Since this is one of relatively few laymen's hymns, it is a peculiarly appropriate tribute to the "laymen" of old, the Wise Men of the East, by a young layman of the West.

Each stanza draws a picture of some detail of the story. Stanza one portrays the joy of the Magi, followed by a prayer to be led as they were.

Stanza two asserts their joyous approach to the manger (not quite in line with the Biblical record, see Matt. 2:11) and a prayer that our feet may willingly approach the mercy seat.

Stanza three portrays the presentation of the gifts; then the prayer that we may bring to Christ our costliest treasures.

Stanza four contains a broader prayer that we may be kept in the Way and find entrance into glory.

The tune "Dix" first appeared in 1838 in a collection of chorales edited and published by Conrad Kocher (1786–1872), organist of the Stiftskirche, Stuttgart, 1827–1865. While the tune was distasteful to the author of the hymn ("I dislike it, but now nothing will displace it"), it came to be associated inseparably with the words and may be said to be strong, vital, joyous, and to have the tread of a stately procession.

---

5   *Away in a Manger*

Anonymous   Probably arranged by
                                           James R. Murray, 1841–c.1904

Away in a manger,
   No crib for a bed,
The little Lord Jesus
   Laid down His sweet head;
The stars in the sky
   Looked down where He lay,

The little Lord Jesus
Asleep on the hay.

The cattle are lowing,
    The poor baby wakes,
But little Lord Jesus
    No crying He makes;
I love Thee, Lord Jesus!
    Look down from the sky,
And stay by my cradle
    Till morning is nigh.

Be near me, Lord Jesus,
    I ask Thee to stay
Close by me forever,
    And love me, I pray.
Bless all the dear children
    In Thy tender care,
And take me to heaven
    To live with Thee there.

(The music is readily available, but the German text is very
rare. Both are printed in *Favorite Christmas, Folk and Sacred
Songs*. The Old Orchard Publishers, Webster Groves, Mo.)

While " Away in a Manger " has frequently been referred to as
Luther's " Cradle Hymn," there is no convincing evidence
that he wrote it. Investigations up to the present seem to be inclined
to the view that the colony of German Lutherans in Pennsylvania
was responsible for its origin and wide popularity in America, and
that it was taken to England a little later, where it is very popular
today. Its popularity in America was no doubt aided by the association of the carol with a picture depicting Luther and his family
at Christmas, painted by Gustave F. L. Koenig and included in

T. B. Stork's *Luther's Christbaum,* published in Philadelphia in 1855.

Richard S. Hill, in an amusing article "Not so Far Away in a Manger — Forty-one Settings of an American Carol" (*Notes,* December, 1945, Second Series, III, No. 1, published by the Music Library Association), traced the appearance of the first two stanzas to a *Little Children's Book,* published in 1885, under the auspices of the Evangelical Lutheran Church in North America. Here the verses were unattributed and set to an obscure hymn, "St. Kilda," by J. E. Clark. Two years later James R. Murray, in *Dainty Songs for Little Lads and Lasses,* called the poem "Luther's Cradle Hymn, composed by Martin Luther for his children, and still sung by German mothers to their little ones." Mr. Hill, quoted above, believes that certain clues indicate that the verses were printed separately without a musical setting, in a quasi-fictional play or story for children about the life of Martin Luther.

It is quite possible, then, that the song was known in Pennsylvania by 1855 in English and came to be associated by the Lutherans there with Luther, leading naturally to a translation into the German since that language was commonly used in the church services, Sunday schools, and for Christmas programs of that day.

The author of this volume ran across a German translation of this beloved Christmas lullaby and reprinted it in a collection of German-English Christmas songs in 1934, ascribing it uncritically to Luther. That German text was reprinted in *Favorite Christmas, Folk and Sacred Songs* in 1948.

That the above viewpoint as to the history of this carol seems essentially correct is further indicated by the fact that, while it is used much in the U. S. and in England, it is practically unknown in Germany. Had Luther written it, it would certainly have been used by his people through the centuries along with his other songs. Personal letters and inquiries through newspapers and periodicals of wide circulation in Germany have brought only references to versions in English-speaking countries, save one lone German translation (besides the one mentioned above), namely, a version that is included in a volume in the German language — *Europaeische Weihnachtslieder,* compiled by Adolf Strube and published by the Carl Merseburger

Verlag, Berlin and Darmstadt. We owe part of the above information to Renate Deppe of the Overseas Department of the Evangelical Church of Germany at Stuttgart.

The most popular musical setting seems to come to us from J. R. Murray (c.1887); in 1921 this tune was ascribed to a Carl Mueller without verification. The second setting, "Afton Water," is, of course, familiar from "Flow Gently, Sweet Afton," by J. E. Spilman.

The verses of this carol reflect clearly Saint Francis' attempt in 1223 to humanize and vitalize the Christmas story through dramatizing it by means of the manger and the events associated with it. Of the many charming manger carols and lullabies that resulted, this one is possibly the most beloved, and its beautiful flowing melody and appealing pictures in the text suggest the very rocking of a cradle. It is one of the purest lullaby carols, gentle in rhythm and quiet in tone.

Even as the author, the composer, and the origin of the first two stanzas are obscure, so the origin of the third stanza, though supposedly of comparatively recent origin, remains uncertain. Bishop William F. Anderson ascribed it to a Dr. John T. McFarland in the period 1904–1908; but it was already included in *Gabriel's Vineyard Songs* in 1892. Therefore it apparently was added during the years between 1855 and 1892 by an anonymous author.

---

6 *The Boar's Head Carol*

Traditional English

Possibly by
Wynkyn de Worde, 1521

> The boar's head in hand bear I,
> Bedecked with bays and rosemary.
> And I pray you, my masters, be merry,
> Quot estis in convivio.
>> *Caput apri defero*
>> *Reddens laudes Domino.*

The boar's head, I understand,
The finest dish in all the land.
Which is thus all bedecked with gay garland,
    Let us servire cantico.

The Boar's Head Carol is the oldest secular carol in existence. A single leaf of the earliest printed collection of carols made in 1521 in England has survived to this day, and on this leaf is this ancient song.

Wild boars were plentiful in England in Druid days, often being offered in sacrifice by priests to the goddess Frigga. The boar was revered by these people as having suggested the idea of plowing through digging its tusks into the earth.

The serving of the boar's head with great fanfare at the Christmas feast is based on a famous legend of a Queen's College student who, while studying his Aristotle, was attacked by a wild boar. Having no weapon of defense, the student crammed the book down the boar's throat. The boar's head was then prepared and served to all the students amid much rejoicing. Ever since, the boar's head has been served at Queen's College in the Christmas season.

This college custom was soon taken up by English rulers and by the nobility and then became a tradition and a favorite Christmas rite. A great ceremony is made of bringing in the boar's head (now a false head with a piece of brown paper under it), and as a part of it the Boar's Head Carol is sung by a single voice. As the platter advances, everyone joins in the chorus.

The words "bedecked with bays and rosemary" refer to popular Christmas decorations. Legend says that rosemary was named after the Virgin and symbolized the purple cloak she wore on the flight to Egypt. It was formerly white, but as the Holy Family rested by the wayside, Mary placed her cloak over a rosemary bush and the color changed to purple.

Both words and music are generally regarded as traditional but some authorities are inclined to credit the music to Wynkyn de Worde, of whom nothing else is known.

7 Brahms's Cradle Song (Christmas Version)

Tr. by Karl Simrock, 1802–1876   Johannes Brahms, 1833–1897
Christmas version tr. by Arthur Westbrook; alt. by H. H. W.

Lullaby and good night!
With roses bedight,
Creep into thy bed,
There pillow thy head.
Lay thee down now and rest,
With purest slumber be blest.
Lay thee down now and rest,
With purest slumber be blest.

Lullaby and good night!
Those blue eyes close tight,
Bright angels are near,
So sleep without fear.
They will guard thee from harm,
With fair dreamland's sweet charm.
They will guard thee from harm,
With fair dreamland's sweet charm.

The Christmas idea appears in stanza one of the original German, translated as follows:

Lullaby and good night!
With angels in sight;
For you'll surely see
Christ-child's Christmas tree.
Sleep then, resting in peace,
Dream of Paradise sweet;
Sleep then, resting in peace,
Dream of Paradise sweet.

(Music, German and English texts in *Favorite Christmas, Folk and Sacred Songs*. The Old Orchard Publishers, Webster Groves, Mo.)

Bishop Reginald Heber was born in Malpas, England, April 21, 1783. Even in childhood his poetic gifts were evident, and at Oxford he was a student of distinction. Through his Bampton lectures on the Holy Spirit in 1815, together with his sermons, hymns, and poems, he gave evidence of being an intellectual as well as a spiritual leader.

After he was made Bishop of Calcutta in 1822, he concluded his literary work and devoted himself to missionary travel and service. Exhausted by fever and arduous labor, he died suddenly on April 3, 1826, after having baptized forty-two persons that day. Had he done nothing beyond leaving behind the notable hymns " The Son of God Goes Forth to War," " From Greenland's Icy Mountains," " Holy, Holy, Holy! " and the one being discussed, his immortality in the hearts of men would be assured.

The hymn before us is perhaps the first he wrote. It was published in the *Christian Observer* for November, 1811. Heber's poems gave offense to certain narrow-minded devout folks who felt that this hymn bordered on star-worshiping and that the rhythm was too dancelike. He replied that in his hymns " no fulsome or indecorous language has been knowingly adopted; no erotic addresses to Him whom no unclean lips can approach; no allegory ill understood and worse applied." His deep spirituality and his self-sacrificing devotion speak even more loudly.

The hymn was written on Epiphany Sunday, that is, on or near January 6, in line with Bishop Heber's principles that hymns should be liturgical and follow the Church year. The gospel to be read on that day is Matt. 2:1-12.

The first stanza centers our interest upon the star, here personified as a " son of the morning." While the reference is primarily to the star the Wise Men saw (Matt. 2:1-10), the Redeemer is also symbolized by the " bright and morning star " (Rev. 22:16).

In stanza two the poet's imagination sees the dewdrops on the cradle and the beasts of the stall, as well as the angels adoring the " Maker and Monarch and Saviour of all." In stanza three we (the singers) become the worshiping kings; the original frankincense becomes " odors of Edom "; the forest and mine provide the myrrh and the gold; while gems and pearls are added for good measure.

Stanza four points out that more costly and precious than these gifts are the "heart's adoration" and "the prayers of the poor."

The first stanza often is repeated as stanza five, thus offering a fitting conclusion in uttering the prayer that the star may dawn on our darkness and guide us to our Redeemer.

> Brightest and best of the sons of the morning,
>> Dawn on our darkness, and lend us Thine aid;
> Star of the East, the horizon adorning,
>> Guide where our infant Redeemer is laid.

While the hymn is at times used with the tune "Wesley," written by Lowell Mason (used with "Hail to the Brightness of Zion's Glad Morning!"), it is more commonly sung to "Morning Star," composed in 1892 by James P. Harding for use in the Gifford Hall Mission in one of the worst slum districts in London. This tune was introduced into the United States in *The New Psalms and Hymns,* Richmond, Virginia, 1901, through a Southern Presbyterian collection. In 1905 it was the setting for this hymn in *The Methodist Hymnal.* Its brightness and carol-like quality have gained for it a permanent place. It should not be sung too rapidly, but rather with a flowing smoothness.

---

9 Bring a Torch, Jeannette, Isabella!

Traditional   Traditional

> Bring a torch, Jeannette, Isabella!
> Bring a torch, to the cradle run!
> It is Jesus, good folk of the village,
> Christ is born and Mary's calling.
> Ah! ah! beautiful is the mother;
> Ah! ah! beautiful is her Son!
>
> It is wrong when the Child is sleeping,
> It is wrong to talk so loud;
> Silence, all, as you gather around,

Lest your noise should waken Jesus:
Hush! hush! see how fast He slumbers;
Hush! hush! see how fast He sleeps!

Softly to the little stable,
Softly for a moment come;
Look and see how charming is Jesus,
How He is white, His cheeks are rosy!
Hush! hush! see how the Child is sleeping;
Hush! hush! see how He smiles in dreams!

While both words and music are regarded by many as traditional, some scholars attribute this charming carol to Nicholas Saboly (1614–1675).

The song describes very beautifully the Christmas Eve celebration as observed by families of Provence, France, in the seventeenth century. Its warmhearted expression of the Christmas spirit is responsible for its continued popularity.

The French people at that period, as in many cases today, celebrated the crèche or manger scene with quite elaborate festivities. At midnight on Christmas Eve everyone lighted a torch or candle and joined the Christmas procession, greeting friends with the words, "Jesus has come." Singing of noels and the ringing of bells added joy to the colorful occasion.

The verses quoted above are the translation ascribed to Edward Cathbert Nunn. Born in Bristol, England, February 23, 1868, he was an organist, composer, and conductor. He died in London, November 26, 1914.

Some see in the expression "Bring a torch" an allusion to an element in the ancient Jewish Festival of Lights — now commonly called Hanukkah — which included a torchlight procession.

At any rate, it can be called a genuine torch song, albeit not in the twentieth century sense!

10 The Cherry Tree Carol

(Joseph Was an Old Man)

Traditional

Joseph was an old man,
  An old man was he:
He married sweet Mary,
  The Queen of Galilee.

As they went awalking,
  In the garden so gay,
Maid Mary spied cherries,
  Hanging over yon tree.

Mary said to Joseph
  With her sweet lips so mild,
" Pluck those cherries, Joseph,
  For to give to my Child."

" O then," replied Joseph
  With words so unkind,
" I will pluck no cherries
  For to give to thy Child."

Mary said to cherry tree,
  " Bow down to my knee,
That I may pluck cherries
  By one, two, and three."

The uppermost sprig then
  Bowed down to her knee:
" Thus you may see, Joseph,
  These cherries are for me."

Traditional

" O eat your cherries, Mary,
  O eat your cherries now,
O eat your cherries, Mary,
  That grow upon the bough."

As Joseph was awalking
  He heard angels sing,
" This night there shall be born
  Our heavenly King.

" He neither shall be born
  In house nor in hall,
Nor in the place of paradise,
  But in an ox stall.

" He shall not be clothed
  In purple nor pall;
But all in fair linen,
  As wear babies all.

"He shall not be rocked,
  In silver nor gold,
But in a wooden cradle
  That rocks on the mould.

" He neither shall be christened
  In white wine nor in red,
But in pure spring well water
  As we were christenèd."

Mary took her Baby,
　She dressed Him so sweet,
She laid Him in a manger
　All there for to sleep.

As she stood over Him
　She heard angels sing,
"Oh! bless our dear Saviour,
Our heavenly King."

This traditional carol goes back some five hundred years or more. While most closely related to England in recent centuries, where we find it in the Coventry mystery plays of the sixteenth century, Rev. Sabine Baring-Gould of England found traces of cherry tree legends in Mexican mythology and in hieroglyphics recently discovered in Egyptian tombs. Dr. Philips of Oxford states that the legend is well known also in France, where it is, however, applied to an apple tree.

According to the legend, Joseph, as an old man, is walking to Bethlehem with his young bride, Mary, "in a garden gay, where cherries were growing on every spray," and she tells him of the visits of the angel. As doubt enters his mind, Joseph is filled with a jealous rage, and he refuses to pick the cherries for his wife.

But the tree, hearing Mary's request, itself bends graciously over and gives her of its fruits. Joseph then knows that he should not have refused to pick the cherries and falls on his knees to ask forgiveness for his unjust suspicions.

At first the legend was perpetuated in the form of a mystery play. By 1833 the words were set to a melody, possibly a folk tune, and were published in William Sandys' *Christmas Carols, Ancient and Modern*. Since that time the carol has been sung in England and many other countries every Christmas season.

---

11 The Christmas Tree, the Fairest Tree

Attrib. to J. Karl   German Folk Song

The Christmas tree, the fairest tree,
  On earth no rival knowing;
However small the garden be,
All radiant blooms the wondrous tree,
  With every flower glowing,
  With every flower glowing, yes, glowing.

List while I tell: One glorious night,
  The Lord to earth was given —
The Saviour who, with holy light,
Led lost and sinful man aright
  And brought him back to heaven,
  And brought him back to heaven, to heaven.

His gracious rays illume the earth,
  The night of fear dispelling,
Your Christmas gifts, your joyous mirth
Today the Christ-child sends to earth.
  Come make your heart His dwelling.
  Come make your heart His dwelling, His dwelling.

O let Him in! 'tis not a dream;
  Your heart shall be His garden,
Wherein shall grow a tree most fair,
Protected by His tender care,
  And yielding peace and pardon,
  And yielding peace and pardon, and pardon.

(Music and German text available in *Favorite Christmas,
Folk and Sacred Songs.* The Old Orchard Publishers, Webster
Groves, Mo.)

This song is one of two in this book that were inspired by the Christmas tree. (See No. 37, "O Christmas Tree," for more extensive notes on the introduction of the tree into the Christmas festivities.) The words are attributed to a J. Karl, of whom nothing further is known.

The tune is, as we have found so frequently the case with older carols especially, an old folk melody.

Those readers who can follow both the German and the English texts will recognize the translation as accurate and beautiful at the same time.

While "O Christmas Tree" ("O Tannenbaum") has only a very faint religious message, this song contains, especially in stanzas two to four, a positive Christian note based on the Nativity story in Luke.

Though it is regrettable that we do not know more about the author and know nothing about the composer nor of the translator, the intrinsic beauty of both music and message should, in time, make this song more popular than its rival referred to above.

---

12 Come, All Ye Shepherds

Bohemian Folk Song   Bohemian Folk Song
Tr. Mari Ruef Hofer, 1912

Come, all ye shepherds, ye children of earth,
Come ye, bring greetings to yon heavenly birth.
For Christ the Lord to all men is given,
To be our Saviour sent down from heaven:
    Come, welcome Him!

Hasten, then, hasten to Bethlehem's stall,
There to see heaven descend to us all.
With holy feeling, there humbly kneeling,
We will adore Him, bow down before Him,
    Worship the King.

Angels and shepherds together we go,
Seeking this Saviour from all earthly woe;
While angels, winging, His praise are singing,
Heaven's echoes ringing, peace on earth bringing,
Good will to men.

(Music in *The Hymnal*, Evangelical and Reformed Church;
The Mennonite Hymnary.)

Here we have a shepherd carol from Bohemia, a land now incorporated into Czechoslovakia. Words and music are traditional.
While there are hymn collections of the Bohemian-Moravian Brethren that can be traced back to 1500 and earlier, this carol seems to be of recent origin. At least so far it has been found only in compilations of folklore of Czechoslovakia that approach the twentieth century. In a 576-page *Bibliographie des deutschen Volksliedes in Boehmen,* published in Prague in 1913, No. 705, p. 125, it appears as "Kommet, kommet, Ihr Hirten," and originated, according to Dr. Gustav Jungbauer, the most notable compiler and editor of such literature, in the Bohemian Wiesenthal.

The translator apparently used this text and others (e.g., *Deutsche Volkslieder aus Boehmen,* ed. by Alois Hruschka and Wendelin Toischer, published in Prague, 1891) in preparing her very free version.

To indicate how free a translation we have in our present version, practically a paraphrase, we quote two stanzas of the original text compiled by Dr. Jungbauer (as they appeared in the *Erzgebirgszeitung,* a newspaper published in the mountain area of Bohemia) on file in the Cleveland Public Library:

Kommet, kommet, Ihr Hirten, kommet alle zugleich,
Nehmet Eure Schalmeien und Pfeifen zu Euch!
Kommet alle zumal in's Freudenreich, in den Stall,
Nach Bethlehem zum Kindelein, zum Jesulein im Stall.

Ein Kindlein zu sehen, wie ein Engel so schoen
Daneben ein alter Vater thut steh'n;
Eine Jungfrau schoen zart, nach engelischer Art,
Es hat sich erfreut ganz jaemmerlich da.

This carol describes the manger scene, portraying Jesus as delicately cared for and the shepherds watching their flocks on Bethlehem's plains. Then the shepherds leave their flocks and go to "see this thing which is come to pass" (Luke 2:15).

The carol is increasingly becoming a favorite of young people in high school and in caroling groups, and is winning its way into the hymnals of our churches.

---

13 Come Hither, Ye Children

(O Come, Little Children)

Christoph von Schmidt, 1768–1854   J. A. P. Schulz, 1747–1800
Tr. Anonymous

Come hither, ye children, O come one and all,
To Bethlehem hasten, in manger so small.
God's Son for a gift has been sent you this night,
To be your Redeemer, your joy and delight.

O see, in the manger, this strange little bed,
The Son, sweet and gentle, is resting His head.
In swaddling clothes lying so meek and so mild,
Yet purer than angels, the heavenly Child.

On hay and on straw in the manger He lies;
Both Mary and Joseph, with fond loving eyes,
Are gazing upon it, and shepherds draw near,
And jubilant angels from heaven appear.

O kneel with the shepherds in worshipful prayer,
And join the dear angels who also are there;
Sing glory to God in the heavens above,
And praise Him for Jesus, the gift of His love.

(Music, English and German texts available in *Favorite Christmas, Folk and Sacred Songs*. The Old Orchard Publishers, Webster Groves, Mo.)

Children who are introduced to this hymn greatly enjoy singing it because of both its vivid imagery and its lively tempo.

The author, Christoph von Schmidt, was born in Dinkelsbühl, Germany, the oldest son of a city clerk, in 1768 and died in Augsburg in 1854. In 1791 he was ordained to the ministry and was given the headship of the school and made school inspector in a small town called Thannhausen.

His fruitful ministry was specially directed toward the needs of young people. He used the early morning hours, four to eight, in writing for them — the only hours he considered his own. As a child of ten years he was greatly impressed with the Nativity scenes that were placed in the corridors of his home church. The vivid recollection of this childhood experience finds picturesque expression in the beloved song for children.

The melody was composed by Johann Abraham Peter Schulz. He was born in Lüneberg, Germany, March 30, 1747. At the age of fifteen he went to Berlin where he studied under Kirnberger, an organist who had been a pupil of Johann Sebastian Bach. Later he traveled in various countries in Europe, resulting in his appointment as band director to the king of Denmark for eight years. He returned to Germany in his later years and died in 1800.

The words of the song appeared in the second edition of *Christliche Gesaenge zur Oeffentlichen Gottesverehrung*, Augsburg, 1811. They naturally are dated some years earlier, but their exact date is not known.

14 Come, Thou Long-expected Jesus

Charles Wesley, 1744
Hyfrydol
Rowland Hugh Prichard, 1855

Come, Thou long-expected Jesus,
  Born to set Thy people free;
From our fears and sins release us;
  Let us find our rest in Thee.
Israel's Strength and Consolation,
  Hope of all the earth Thou art;
Dear Desire of every nation,
  Joy of every longing heart.

Born Thy people to deliver,
  Born a child, and yet a King,
Born to reign in us forever,
  Now Thy gracious Kingdom bring.
By Thine own eternal Spirit
  Rule in all our hearts alone;
By Thine all-sufficient merit
  Raise us to Thy glorious throne.

(Music in the Methodist and Presbyterian hymnals.)

Charles Wesley was born December 18, 1707, the son of Rev. Samuel Wesley, a clergyman in the Church of England. One of nineteen children, Charles attended Oxford University with his older brother John, where they were active in a religious organization which took exception to various practices in the Established Church. Because of their methodical religious habits, the group became known as " Methodists."

Charles Wesley published some four thousand hymns and left two thousand more in manuscript. Authorities differ as to whether he or Isaac Watts was the greater writer of hymns. They were, however, in no sense rivals. Watts emphasized the divine majesty, while Wesley's theme was the love of God. He died in London, March 29, 1788.

Though this hymn was one of the first that Charles Wesley wrote and was published as early as 1744 in a small book of twenty-four pages, *Hymns for the Nativity of Our Lord,* it was not included in the *Wesleyan Hymn Book* before 1875. One reason it was not used more commonly is the fact that it lacked a suitable musical setting before Rowland Prichard's tune "Hyfrydol" was associated with it.

The song is based on Hag. 2:7. It portrays Israel's Messianic reign forever over the hearts of all men.

The tune "Hyfrydol" is a Welsh tune composed in 1855 by Rowland Prichard (1811–1887), of Bala, Wales, who was a song leader, soloist, and composer. The hymn is also sung to a Dutch traditional melody, "In Babilone."

"Hyfrydol's" marked characteristic is the simplicity of its melody, which, except for one note, is confined to the limits of a fifth, from do to sol. Being a happy tune and at the same time firm and smooth, it is an appropriate setting for this exhilarating hymn.

---

15 Deck the Halls

Traditional   Old Welsh Air

Deck the halls with boughs of holly,
Fa la la la la, la la la la.
'Tis the season to be jolly,
Fa la la la la, la la la la.
Don we now our gay apparel,
Fa la la, la la la, la la la,
Troll the ancient Yuletide carol,
Fa la la la la, la la la la.

See the blazing Yule before us,
Strike the harp and join the chorus,
Follow me in merry measure,
While I tell of Yuletide's treasure.

Fast away the old year passes,
Hail the new, ye lads and lasses,
Sing we joyous all together,
Heedless of the wind and weather.

Deck the Halls" is one of the best known secular carols and is a universal favorite in English-speaking lands. The melody is an old traditional one from Wales, once used by Mozart as the theme of a composition for violin and piano.

The song is one of the jolly carols of the Yule celebrations. The words make no reference to the Nativity, but tell us much about the customs of the season of Yule which were taken over from earlier pagan winter festivals.

The most famous of these was the Yule log ("yule" comes from "rol," a wheel that indicated the changing of the seasons). While particularly significant in England, it is also found in Scandinavian countries. The Yule log was cut in the forest amid dancing and singing and then brought into a great hall and lighted with a special musical ceremony.

Sumptuous feasting on plum pudding and mince pies, and drinking from the wassail bowl, lasted as long as the log burned! Among English colonial planters of Virginia and Maryland, the Negro slaves searched for the largest water-soaked logs that the merry season of leisure might last as long as possible.

Throughout Great Britain the halls were trimmed with holly, evergreen, and mistletoe, a custom traceable to the Roman Saturnalia. Later the holly wreath with its prickles and blood-red berries became symbolic of the Saviour's crown of thorns.

"Follow me in merry measure" suggests that the singers would dance about as they sang, much as they would in a ring dance.

---

16 *Everywhere, Everywhere, Christmas Tonight*

Bishop Phillips Brooks, 1835–1893   Lewis H. Redner, 1831–1908

Christmas in lands of the fir tree and pine,
Christmas in lands of the palm tree and vine,
Christmas where snow peaks stand solemn and white,
Christmas where cornfields lie sunny and bright,
Everywhere, everywhere, Christmas tonight.

Christmas where children are hopeful and gay,
Christmas where old men are patient and gray,
Christmas where peace like a dove in its flight
Broods o'er brave men in the thick of the fight,
Everywhere, everywhere, Christmas tonight.

(Music available in *Noëls,* H. T. FitzSimons Company, Chicago, Ill.; *Christmas in Song,* Rubank, Inc., Chicago, Ill.)

For the author, Phillips Brooks, and the composer, Lewis Redner, see " O Little Town of Bethlehem," No. 41.

This inspiring song by Phillips Brooks ranks second only, among his poems, to the immortal favorite, " O Little Town of Bethlehem." It reflects the universal spirit of Christmas in a splendid manner.

The esteem in which Brooks was held by old and young alike is reflected beautifully in a rare, all-inclusive tribute paid him by a girl of five, who, when told by her mother that the beloved bishop had died, exclaimed, " Mother, how happy the angels will be!" That which made him so beloved in his day and likewise caused his hymns and poems as well as his sermons to live on, was his fervent evangelical faith. He came to Trinity Church at a time when Boston was the center of the Unitarian movement. Many were, however, beginning to turn from this austere intellectualism to the warmhearted gospel of a divine Saviour. One person put it into these simple words: " I have never heard preaching like it. . . . I was electrified; I could have got up and shouted."

Harvard-trained, of great intellectual ability, his life and ministry centering in Christ, Brooks presented Him not as a wrathful judge but as the loving Redeemer. Beautifully this is reflected in another of his carols. We have room for only a few stanzas:

The earth has grown cold with its burden of care,
  But at Christmas it always is young,
The heart of the jewel burns lustrous and fair,
And its soul full of music breaks forth on the air,
  When the song of the angels is sung.

" It is coming, old earth, it is coming tonight,
  On the snowflakes which cover thy sod,
The feet of the Christ-child fall gently and white,
And the voice of the Christ-child tells out with delight
  That mankind are the children of God.

" On the sad and the lonely, the wretched and poor,
  That voice of the Christ-child shall fall;
And to every blind wanderer opens the door
Of a hope which he dared not to dream of before,
  With a sunshine of welcome for all.

" The feet of the humblest may walk in the field
  Where the feet of the holiest have trod,
This, this is the marvel of mortals revealed,
When the silvery trumpets of Christmas have pealed,
  That mankind are the children of God."

That same thought and spirit are beautifully expressed in the statue erected in front of Trinity Church, Boston, as a memorial. Behind the stalwart figure of the preacher, stands the Christ, the source of his constant inspiration.

———

17 *Fairest Lord Jesus!*

(Beautiful Saviour)

German, 17th century

Silesian Folk Song Melody
Arr. Richard S. Willis, 1850

Fairest Lord Jesus!
Ruler of all nature!
　　O Thou of God and man the Son!
Thee will I cherish,
Thee will I honor,
　　Thou, my soul's glory, joy, and crown!

Fair are the meadows,
Fairer still the woodlands,
　　Robed in the blooming garb of spring:
Jesus is fairer,
Jesus is purer,
　　Who makes the woeful heart to sing.

Fair is the sunshine,
Fairer still the moonlight,
　　And all the twinkling, starry host:
Jesus shines brighter,
Jesus shines purer,
　　Than all the angels heaven can boast!

While this is not distinctly a Christmas hymn, its central emphasis on Jesus makes it appropriate for any of the great Church festivals, and hence it is used frequently at the time of the commemoration of his Nativity.

For some time it was known as the "Crusaders' Hymn," but there is no real foundation for the tradition that it was sung by the German knights of the twelfth century on their way to Jerusalem. Even though it is agreed quite largely that both text and tune are more modern, we do not know who translated it into our present English form.

There seems to be quite convincing evidence that the German text was published in the *Muenster Songbook* in 1677; that our English translation is by an unknown translator; that a later translation, beginning "Beautiful Saviour," was made by Joseph A. Seiss of Maryland in 1873.

The beautiful melody, though a common folk tune, cannot be traced back beyond 1842 when it was first printed in *Silesian Folk Songs* in Leipzig, having been committed to paper in the province of Glatz (a town in Silesia just over the border a hundred miles east by north from Prague, the home of John Hus, the noted Protestant Reformer in Bohemia) as a result of the joint labors of August Heinrich Hoffman von Fallersleben (1798–1874) and Ernst Friedrich Richter (1809–1879).

English-language congregations were first introduced to the hymn and tune in 1850 when Richard Storrs Willis harmonized the melody and included it in his publication, *Church Chorals and Choir Studies.*

This "unexpected treasure" reflects vividly the background indicated above. It expresses the appreciation of the fair objects in nature along with the fairest Person known by the peasant folk of Silesia. They saw in Jesus a Son of both God and man (stanza one) who, while ruling all nature, was yet fairer than all.

The hymn beautifully observes the meadows, the woodlands, the sunshine, the moonlight, and the stars in their radiant beauty, along with the simplicity of thought about Jesus that is appealing to the child and yet at the same time challenging to the grownup.

It can be used effectively as the central theme of a worship service by reading as an introduction to the first stanza John 1:1-4. With the second stanza, Emerson's poem "Music" will be helpful:

> It is not only in the rose,
> It is not only in the bird,
> Not only where the rainbow glows,
> Nor in the song of woman heard,
> But in the darkest, meanest things
> There alway, alway something sings.

(Copyright, Houghton Mifflin Company. Used by permission.)

The third stanza supplements beautifully Ps. 8, often called the "Midnight Hymn":

> When I consider thy heavens, the work of thy fingers,
> The moon and the stars, which thou hast ordained;
> What is man, that thou art mindful of him?
> And the son of man, that thou visitest him?
> For thou hast made him a little lower than the angels,
> And hast crowned him with glory and honor.
>
> — Ps. 8:3-5.

After being reminded of the majestic, entrancing beauties of nature's wonders on earth and in the skies, Jesus towers over all "brighter," "fairer," "purer, than all the angels heaven can boast."

This song can be used with good effect both as a solo with humming accompaniment and in four-part harmony. Dr. F. Melius Christiansen, who directed the noted St. Olaf College Choir (Minnesota) has arranged an anthem on this melody using the words "Beautiful Saviour."

---

18 *The First Nowel*

English Carol, 17th century   Traditional melody in
                                W. Sandys' *Christmas Carols*, 1833

> The first Nowel the angels did say
> Was to certain poor shepherds in fields as they lay,
> In fields where they lay a-keeping their sheep,
> On a cold winter's night that was so deep.
>   *Nowel, Nowel, Nowel, Nowel,*
>   *Born is the King of Israel!*
>
> They looked up and saw a star
> Shining in the east beyond them far,
> And to the earth it gave great light,
> And so it continued both day and night.

And by the light of that same star,
Three Wise Men came from a country afar;
To seek for a king was their intent
And to follow the star wherever it went.

This star drew nigh to the northwest;
O'er Bethlehem it took its rest,
And there it did both stop and stay,
Right over the place where Jesus lay.

Then entered in those Wise Men three
Full reverently upon their knee,
And offered there in His presence
Their gold, and myrrh, and frankincense.

Then let us all with one accord
Sing praises to our heavenly Lord;
That hath made heaven and earth of naught,
And with His blood mankind hath bought.

This English carol of the seventeenth century has been deservedly popular. It gives a purely narrative song on a level that children can comprehend. The word "carol" is derived from "carola," a ring dance. Being denied the opportunity to sing in the churches, the people sang outside. While the people were dancing (caroling), tunes and words were made up by one or more bystanders from the Nativity incidents. This accounts for occasional inaccuracies like the shepherds seeing the star.

Authorities disagree as to whether this song comes from France or England. The French "Noël" (English "Nowel" or "Nowell") may have some association with the Latin "novella" (news), but it more likely came from the Provençal "nadal," a corruption of the Latin "natalis" (birthday). While older versions exist, the form of our present text dates back to William Sandys' *Christmas Carols, Ancient and Modern,* 1833.

The *first* Nowel reminds us that carol singing is not a twentieth century innovation, or even a medieval custom, but goes all the way back to the Nativity itself. Immediately after the time of the New Testament, in 129, as mentioned in No. 3, "Angels We Have Heard on High," we read of Telesphorus, bishop of Rome, inaugurating the custom of celebrating the Nativity with the singing of carols. And in that connection we are told that a song never to be omitted was that of the angels, "Glory to God in the highest," truly the very first Christmas song.

The "First Nowel" we have before us is in the form of a medieval shepherd song, noted for its simplicity. It has been called rhymed prose, carried along and made popular by the sweep of its music.

---

19 *From Heaven Above*

Martin Luther, 1535
Tr. by Catherine Winkworth

Geistliche Lieder
Leipzig, 1539

From heaven above to earth I come
To bear good news to every home;
Glad tidings of great joy I bring,
Whereof I now will say and sing:

"To you, this night, is born a Child
Of Mary, chosen mother mild;
This little Child of lowly birth,
Shall be the joy of all the earth.

" 'Tis Christ, our God, who far on high
Hath heard your sad and bitter cry;
Himself will your salvation be,
Himself from sin will make you free."

Welcome to earth, Thou noble guest,
Through whom e'en wicked men are blest!

43

Thou comest to share our misery;
What can we render, Lord, to Thee?

Ah, dearest Jesus, Holy Child,
Make Thee a bed, soft, undefiled,
Within my heart that it may be
A quiet chamber kept for Thee!

Glory to God in highest heaven,
Who unto men His Son hath given,
While angels sing with pious mirth
A glad New Year to all the earth.

(Music with English and German texts available in *Favorite Christmas, Folk and Sacred Songs*. The Old Orchard Publishers, Webster Groves, Mo.)

Early Christmas Eve, 1534, sitting beside the cradle of his little son Paul, Luther takes down his lute and begins to hum and sing. His thoughts are guided to the popular folk tune, "From Foreign Lands I Have Come Here," and he uses this as a pattern to sing to little Paul the Christmas story of Luke, ch. 2. He writes and revises the stanzas and finally there are fifteen.

It is said that in succeeding years Luther celebrated the festival by having the first seven stanzas sung by a man dressed as an angel. Then the children joyfully responded by singing the remaining stanzas and on the last stanza all would leap into a gleeful dance.

The song was first published in Wittenberg in 1535. The tune now associated with it appeared in 1539, possibly composed by Luther himself. In 1543 words and tune appeared in *Klug's Hymnbook* with the subtitle "A Children's Hymn of the Christ-child for Christmas Eve." The hymn continues to be sung from the domes of churches in Germany, before daybreak on Christmas morning.

Present-day translations are based largely on Catherine Winkworth's version in *Lyra Germanica,* first series, 1855. This noted translator made a special study of German hymns and hymn writers and became the foremost scholar in making available in English the noted German chorales and hymns.

20 Go, Tell It on the Mountains

Negro Spiritual   Negro Spiritual

When I was a learner, I sought both night and day,
I asked the Lord to aid me and He showed me the way.
Go, tell it on the mountains,
Over the hills an' everywhere,
Go, tell it on the mountains,
Our Jesus Christ is born.
> *Go over the hills an' everywhere,*
> *Go, tell it on the mountains, Go!*

He made me a watchman upon the city wall
An' if I am a Christian I am the least of all.
Go, tell it on the mountains,
Over the hills an' everywhere,
Go, tell it on the mountains,
Our Jesus Christ is born.

The influence of Christmas customs is reflected in the songs of Negro slaves that have come down to us in the form of Negro spirituals or "songs of the spirit." The Negro needs no audience, for he sings many of the songs to himself; sometimes he addresses them to God, thus establishing a close relationship that gives him the feeling that God is near and ready to help at all times.

The spirituals, particularly those with the Christmas message, are as simple as the humble, crude surroundings in which the Negroes were born and lived. Many came from the lips of slave mothers while they nursed their babies.

Of the few that are available we have chosen " Go, Tell It on the Mountains " as one with a commonplace air, but filled with glory and might in both melody and message.

---

21 *God Rest You Merry, Gentlemen*

English Traditional   English Traditional Melody
                                       Harm. by Sir John Stainer, 1867

God rest you merry, gentlemen,
  Let nothing you dismay,
Remember Christ our Saviour
  Was born on Christmas Day,
To save us all from Satan's power
  When we were gone astray.
    O tidings of comfort and joy,
    Comfort and joy;
    O tidings of comfort and joy.

From God our Heavenly Father
  A blessed angel came,
And unto certain shepherds
  Brought tidings of the same,
How that in Bethlehem was born
  The Son of God by name.

" Fear not, then," said the angel,
  " Let nothing you affright,
This day is born a Saviour
  Of a pure Virgin bright,
To free all those who trust in Him
  From Satan's power and might."

Now to the Lord sing praises,
  All you within this place,

And with true love and brotherhood
Each other now embrace;
This holy tide of Christmas
All others doth deface.

"God Rest You Merry, Gentlemen" is the most popular carol in England, containing a joyous note of Christmas cheer from "Merrie" England. The verses of this quaint carol relate the story in a childlike but very touching manner.

The opening line is frequently misunderstood, because too often the comma is omitted after "merry." "God rest you merry" means "May God keep you merry, O gentlemen."

The carol is so full of Christian joy that it is almost boisterous in its meter. Because of this characteristic, the music is cheerful enough to suit the words in spite of its minor key.

It breathes a beautiful humility before the mystery of Him who was born of the Virgin. It is a hymn of good fellowship celebrating the joyous companionship of those who know the power of God that came to expression in the manger.

Charles Dickens, in his immortal *Christmas Carol*, portrays how the words "God rest you merry, gentlemen" caused Scrooge to seize "the ruler with such energy of action that the singer fled in terror."

The tune is an English traditional melody, harmonized by Sir John Stainer (1840–1901), a prolific composer.

---

22   *Good Christian Men, Rejoice*

In Dulci Jubilo

Medieval Latin
Tr. by John M. Neale, 1853

14th century German melody
Harm. by Sir John Stainer, 1867

Good Christian men, rejoice
With heart and soul and voice;
Give ye heed to what we say:
Jesus Christ is born today;
Man and beast before Him bow,

And He is in the manger now.
Christ is born today!
Christ is born today!

Good Christian men, rejoice
With heart and soul and voice;
Now ye hear of endless bliss;
Jesus Christ was born for this!
He hath oped the heavenly door,
And man is blessed evermore.
Christ was born for this!
Christ was born for this!

Good Christian men, rejoice
With heart and soul and voice;
Now ye need not fear the grave:
Jesus Christ was born to save!
Calls you one and calls you all,
To gain His everlasting hall.
Christ was born to save!
Christ was born to save!

This song is frequently referred to as a translation of "In Dulci Jubilo" by John Mason Neale. If it is to be called a translation, it is more accurate to say it is taken from the German version, "Nu singet und seyt fro." It is actually a paraphrase of the original as can clearly be seen when we place a stanza of the original alongside of a literal translation.

In dulci jubilo	In sweet jubilation
Nu singet und seyt fro!	Now sing and be joyful!
Unsers Herzen wonne	The joy of our hearts
Leyt in praesepio	Lies in a manger
Und leuchtet als die Sonne	And shines like the sun
Matris in gremio.	In the lap of his mother.
Alpha es et O!	Thou art Alpha and Omega!

The original carol was in so-called Latin, macaronic, a barbarous mixture — in this case of Latin and German. Comparing the above stanzas with Neale's more finished product we readily see how excellently he caught the inspiration of the original and transformed it so remarkably that it has maintained and is increasing its popularity.

The translator, John Mason Neale, was born in London, January 24, 1818, son of an Evangelical clergyman. At eighteen he entered Cambridge University, where he was a student of rank. In addition to the volume *Hymns of the Eastern Church,* he is to be remembered in connection with such familiar hymns as " Jerusalem the Golden " and " Art Thou Weary, Art Thou Languid," as also the carol " Good King Wenceslas."

This song breathes a note of happy Christian fellowship and an abandon of joy that both children and adults feel vividly. The joyous affirmations of Christ's birth inspire a sense of world-wide fellowship uniting all Christians. And the implications of Christ's birth in victory over the grave, in stanzas two and three, are themes of joy that move the hearts of men whenever they are sung.

---

23   *Good King Wenceslas*

John Mason Neale, 1818–1866

Traditional
Arr. by Sir John Stainer

> Good King Wenceslas looked out
>   On the Feast of Stephen,
> When the snow lay round about,
>   Deep and crisp and even;
> Brightly shone the moon that night,
>   Though the frost was cruel,
> When a poor man came in sight,
>   Gathering winter fuel.
>
> " Hither, page, and stand by me,
>   If thou knowest it, telling;

Yonder peasant, who is he?
    Where and what his dwelling? "
" Sire, he lives a good league hence,
    Underneath the mountain,
Right against the forest fence,
    By Saint Agnes' fountain."

" Bring me flesh, and bring me wine,
    Bring me pine logs hither;
Thou and I will see him dine
    When we bear them thither."
Page and monarch forth they went,
    Forth they went together;
Through the rude wind's wild lament
    And the bitter weather.

" Sire, the night is darker now,
    And the wind blows stronger;
Fails my heart, I know not how,
    I can go no longer."
" Mark my footsteps, my good page,
    Tread thou in them boldly;
Thou shalt find the winter's rage
    Freeze thy blood less coldly."

In his master's steps he trod,
    Where the snow lay dinted;
Heat was in the very sod
    Which the saint had printed.
Therefore, Christian men, be sure,
    Wealth or rank possessing,
Ye who now will bless the poor,
    Shall yourselves find blessing.

Good King Wenceslas " is founded on an old Bohemian legend which tells of King (or Duke) Wenceslas the Holy, who ruled Bohemia A.D. 928–935. He is renowned for his kindness to the poor, especially at Christmas and on St. Stephen's Day, December 26.

The carol is an interesting dialogue between the king and his page. It relates the good deeds of the ruler, how he carries food, drink, and firewood through the dark, snowy night to a peasant's home and ends with the admonition that in blessing the poor, men shall find blessing for themselves.

The tune is that of an old spring carol " Tempus Adest Floridum " (" Spring Has Now Unwrapped the Flowers "), taken from an early Swedish-German hymn collection, *Piae Cantiones,* assembled by Martin Luther but printed after his death. Later John Stainer harmonized the melody. The delightful tune has contributed much to the carol's popularity.

The verses were arranged in dialogue form by John Mason Neale (for biographical note, see No. 22) in the form as we have it. Parts may be assigned to solo voices or the part of the king may be taken in unison by the male voices and the part of the page by the female.

We have here an excellent illustration of the universal appeal of music — in this case, of Christmas music particularly. The melody comes from Sweden, the story from Bohemia (now Czechoslovakia), and the poem from Victorian England.

Its continued popularity is indicated by the fact that in 1929 Czechoslovakia issued a set of postage stamps honoring King Wenceslas. The series shows his portrait, his consecration at the Church of St. Vitus, and his martyrdom.

---

24 *Hark! the Herald Angels Sing*

Charles Wesley, 1739   Felix Mendelssohn, 1840
Arr. by Wm. H. Cummings, 1850

Hark! the herald angels sing,
" Glory to the newborn King;
Peace on earth, and mercy mild,
God and sinners reconciled! "
Joyful, all ye nations, rise,
Join the triumph of the skies;
With the angelic host proclaim,
" Christ is born in Bethlehem! "
     Hark! the herald angels sing,
     " Glory to the newborn King! "

Christ, by highest heaven adored:
Christ, the Everlasting Lord!
Late in time behold Him come
To the earth from heaven's home;
Veiled in flesh the Godhead see;
Hail the incarnate Deity,
Pleased as man with men to dwell,
Jesus, our Emmanuel.

Hail, the heaven-born Prince of Peace!
Hail, the Sun of Righteousness!
Light and life to all He brings,
Risen with healing in His wings.
Mild He lays His glory by,
Born that man no more may die,
Born to raise the sons of earth,
Born to give them second birth.

Here we have another song from the pen of Charles Wesley. Of more than 6,500 that he wrote, this one, along with "Jesus, Lover of My Soul," is among the ten most popular hymns. It was written in his early productive period before 1739, within a year after his conversion, while the spiritual glow remained fresh. On his trip from England to America in 1736, he had so enjoyed hearing some Moravians singing hymns that he was stimulated to his unique work as a writer of religious songs.

This is the only one of the author's many hymns that found its way into the English *Book of Common Prayer*. Because the Wesleys were in disfavor with the Anglican Church, no doubt it was the excellence and the appeal of the song that kept it in that collection and in innumerable collections since.

After having been published in ten four-line stanzas in *Hymns and Sacred Poems* in 1739 shortly after Charles Wesley "consciously believed," it was revised and included in the 1743 edition of the same book under the heading, "Hymn for Christmas Day." George Whitefield included it in his *Collection* in 1753 with the first two lines changed from:

> Hark! how all the welkin rings
> " Glory to the King of Kings "

to the present-day version:

> Hark! the herald angels sing,
> " Glory to the newborn King."

The change was made either by George Whitefield or by a Rev. Martin Madan, the latter having made further changes in the last two lines of the present first stanza (stanza two of the original), making

> Universal nature say,
> " Christ the Lord is born today "

read

> With the angelic hosts proclaim,
> " Christ is born in Bethlehem."

The joyous story of the shepherds, Luke 2:8-14, rings joyfully in the first stanza, as also the message of Isa. 9:6, " Unto us a child is born. . . ." The second stanza refers us to John 1:14, " The Word was made flesh, and dwelt among us." The third stanza praises the Prince of Peace for bringing healing and being " born that man no more may die." Such a wealth and meaning of the Christmas story can come to us only when we hark to the singing of the angels.

Even as the words were subjected to numerous changes, the hymn had been in use one hundred and twenty years before the present tune came to be associated with the words. Only in 1856 did William Haymen Cummings (1831–1915) adapt to this hymn the music from Mendelssohn's " Festgesang, No. 7, Lied 2," which had been composed to celebrate the anniversary of the discovery of printing. Even though Mendelssohn himself said: " It will *never* do to sacred words. There must be a national and merry subject found out, to which the soldierlike motion of the piece has some relation " — it has now become the recognized tune for the hymn. While various names are applied to it, including Berlin, Bethlehem, Jesu Redemptor, St. Vincent, and Nativity, the generally accepted title today is " Mendelssohn."

---

25   *He Became Incarnate*

(An India Christmas Carol)

Tr. by Adele Wobus, 1935   Traditional Melody
and H. H. W.

He became incarnate,
Christ the King of glory.
He became incarnate.

Shepherds were keeping
Their nightly watch on Bethlehem's plain,
Wonderful brightness
Around them shone so marvelously.
" Fear not, O brothers,"

The angel addressed them,
" Joy I proclaim
Through the birth of the Saviour."
 He became incarnate,
 Christ the King of glory.
 He became incarnate.

" This sign I'll show you
By which you'll find the Lord of all,
In David's city
You'll find Him in a lowly stall."
Suddenly heavenly
Hosts sang forth praises,
" Glory to God,
Who gives peace, on earth good will."
 He became incarnate,
 Christ the King of glory.
 He became incarnate.

(Music, English and original texts available in *Carols, Customs and Costumes Around the World.* The Old Orchard Publishers, Webster Groves, Mo.)

This is one of the few Christmas carols available that acquaints us with this ancient Oriental country of India. Even though no pines or cedars grow on the plains of India, the spirit of Christmas has expressed itself in improvised Christmas trees made of bundles of rice straw thickly plastered with mud. Paper chains and mica are scattered over the tree as trimmings.

The music is typical of India, frequent repetition and a narrow range. The melody, after being played and sung repeatedly, has a haunting appeal.

The predominant thought in this carol emphasizes that God came down upon earth and assumed human form. Then the setting from Luke is portrayed (ch. 2): the shepherds on Bethlehem's plain, the

Babe in the lowly stall, and finally the heavenly hosts singing the
" Gloria."

It is doubly interesting to have this characteristic music from India
and the text in the native language.

---

26   Here We Come a-Wassailing [a-Caroling]

Traditional   Old English Melody

Here we come a-wassailing [a-caroling]
    Among the leaves so green;
Here we come a-wandering,
    So fair to be seen.
       Love and joy come to you
       And to you glad Christmas too;
       And God bless you and send you
       A happy New Year,
       And God send you a happy New Year.

We are not daily beggars
    That beg from door to door;
But we are neighbors' children,
    Whom you have seen before.

Good master and mistress,
    As you sit by the fire,
Pray think of us poor children,
    Who wander in the mire.

God bless the master of this house,
    Likewise the mistress too,
And all the little children
    That round the table go.

Here We Come a-Wassailing" appears in many song collections with the last word changed to "a-caroling." It may be sung whichever way it is preferred.

By the fifteenth century caroling was fairly well established in the British Isles, where it displaced the pagan Yule custom of wassailing. The word "wassail" is derived from the Anglo-Saxon "Wase-hael" which signified "Be in health." At the early Saxon feasts, it was the custom to drink a wassail to the lord, and so the wassail bowl became a part of Christmas celebrations.

The drink itself consisted of a combination of mulled ale, eggs, curdled cream, roasted apples, nuts, and spices. It was called "lamb's wool," a corruption of a Celtic word which was applied to any drink in which apples were used.

The wassail bowl is still found in all the great country houses of England and is kept filled from Christmas Eve to Twelfth Night. In some country places the young people go about, offering a hot drink from the wassail bowl and a song in exchange for gifts. Such broad hints as "Pray think of us poor children," can hardly go unheeded.

Quite generally the custom has been displaced by caroling. The gay music, fairly tripping as it goes along, with a slower rhythm in the refrain, has contributed much toward its popularity through the centuries and will no doubt keep it among the dozen best-loved songs for outdoor caroling for years to come.

---

27 The Holly and the Ivy

Traditional English   Old French Melody

The holly and the ivy,
Now both are full well grown,
Of all the trees that are in the wood,
The holly bears the crown.
O the rising of the sun,
The running of the deer,

The playing of the organ,
  Sweet singing in the choir.

The holly bears a blossom
  As white as lily flower;
Mary bore sweet Jesus Christ,
  To be our sweet Saviour.

The holly bears a berry,
  As red as any blood;
And Mary bore sweet Jesus Christ,
  To do poor sinners good.

The holly bears a prickle,
  As sharp as any thorn;
And Mary bore sweet Jesus Christ,
  On Christmas Day in the morn.

The holly bears a bark,
  As bitter as any gall;
And Mary bore sweet Jesus Christ,
  For to redeem us all.

The holly and the ivy
  Now both are full well grown,
Of all the trees that are in the wood,
  The holly bears the crown.

Here we have an old French melody and traditional English words. It is a curious blending of nature worship with the Christian gospel.

The beauties of nature have often inspired certain religious practices that were later completely changed and given a Christian significance. This is vividly true with the fir tree and similarly true with the holly and the ivy.

58

The holly, which grows in some form in almost every country, has been used for festival decorations for centuries. In connection with Christmas it has come to represent the crown of thorns worn by Christ when he was crucified, the red of the berries representing his blood. In many yuletide songs the holly was spoken of as the male and the ivy as the female. The one that was first brought into the house indicated which sex would rule the house that year!

An amusing story embodying this idea is told of an English knight who invited his tenants and their wives to dine with him at Christmas. When the last guest was seated, the knight arose and, with a twinkle in his eye, said to the men, representing the holly, " Before you eat, whoever among you is master of your wife shall now take his stand and carol before the assembly." Finally one timid man arose and sang a short carol.

Then the command was given to the women's table: " Ivy, it is now your turn. Whichever of you is a master of her husband, let her sing a carol as proof." Whereupon "they fell all to such a singing that there was never heard such a caterwauling piece of music." The knight then laughed heartily and shouted merrily, " The ivy, the ivy is the master! "

---

28 *How Lovely Shines the Morning Star!*

(How Brightly Beams the Morning Star)
(O Morning Star, How Fair and Bright)

Philipp Nicolai, 1597   Philipp Nicolai, 1597
Tr. composite

> How lovely shines the Morning Star!
> The nations see and hail afar
>   The light in Judah shining,
> Thou David's Son of Jacob's race,
> My Bridegroom and my King of Grace,
>   For Thee my heart is pining.
>   Lowly, Holy,

Great and glorious,
Thou victorious
Prince of graces,
Filling all the heavenly places.

O highest joy by mortals won,
True Son of God and Mary's Son,
   Thou high-born King of ages!
Thou art my heart's most beauteous Flower,
And Thy blest gospel's saving power
   My raptured soul engages.
      Thou mine, I Thine;
Sing Hosanna!
Heavenly manna
Tasting, eating,
Whilst Thy love in songs repeating.

A pledge of peace from God I see
When Thy pure eyes are turned to me
   To show me Thy good pleasure.
Jesus, Thy Spirit and Thy Word,
Thy body and Thy blood afford
   My soul its dearest treasure.
      Keep me kindly
In Thy favor,
O my Saviour!
Thou wilt cheer me;
Thy Word calls me to draw near Thee.

Oh, joy to know that Thou, my Friend,
Art Lord, Beginning without end,
   The First and Last, Eternal!
And Thou at length, O glorious grace!
Wilt take me to that holy place,

The home of joys supernal.
    Amen, Amen!
Come and meet me!
Quickly greet me!
With deep yearning,
Lord, I look for Thy returning.

(Music available in the Evangelical, Lutheran, and Presbyterian hymnals.)

This powerful song, as regards both tune and content, is known as the " queen of the chorales." The words and music were written in 1597 by the Lutheran pastor Philipp Nicolai, during the same pestilence that inspired him to write " Wake, Awake, for Night Is Flying," generally regarded as the " king of chorales."

While Nicolai was serving a church in Unna, a terrible pestilence claiming over 1,300 victims struck terror into the hearts of the people. The parsonage overlooked the churchyard where as many as thirty burials a day took place. One morning when this tragedy and distress weighed especially heavy upon him, this hymn of the Saviour's love and of the joys of heaven welled forth from his heart. He became so absorbed in it that he forgot his noonday meal and worked on into the late afternoon until the song was completed.

The original German of this hymn was altered seventy years after it was written, and the English translations are varied and free. The first line appears in standard hymnals as " How Brightly Beams the Morning Star," " O Morning Star, How Fair and Bright," " How Bright Appears the Morning Star," and " How Lovely Shines the Morning Star."

It was first published in the author's *Meditations on Eternal Life* in 1599 under the title " A Spiritual Bridal Song of the Believing Soul, Concerning Her Heavenly Bridegroom, Founded on the Forty-fifth Psalm of the Prophet David."

Not only does it contain the note of a spiritual wedding, which caused it to be used at marriages, but its content is so rich that it was used for many other religious occasions as well, particularly Communion services and funerals; and as early as 1610 it was introduced into Sweden where it gained favor especially as an offertory during the Christmas season.

The Christmas note is most clearly evident in the prominence of the Morning Star, an expression recurring in Scripture — Job 38:7; II Peter 1:19; Rev. 22:16. Beyond these Scriptural allusions and the general basis of Ps. 45, the first stanza breathes the spirit of " O Come, O Come, Emmanuel," a Latin hymn of the twelfth century. Stanza two exalts the " Son of God and Mary's Son " (see Col. 1:15 f. and Heb. 1:1, 2). The third stanza implores that the Saviour may come and impart his love, supply his loved ones with his life and cause them to rest in him forever.

Modern collections print five to seven stanzas. The original song ends with the majestic words:

> Sing, ye heavens, tell the story,
> Of His glory,
> Till His praises
> Flood with light earth's darkest places!

So beloved did this song become that its tune was often chimed from city church towers. Lines and stanzas from it were printed by way of ornament on the common earthenware of Germany, and it was invariably used at weddings and on other religious occasions. The excellence of the music, generally known by the first line (" Wie schoen leuchtet der Morgenstern "), is attested by the fact that Mendelssohn used the tune in his " Christus," and Bach made a harmonization of it which appears in his *Vierstimmige Choralgesaenge* and is regarded as one of the most beautiful harmonizations in the field of organ music.

29 I Heard the Bells on Christmas Day

(Christmas Bells)

Henry W. Longfellow, 1863   J. Baptiste Calkin, 1872

I heard the bells on Christmas Day
Their old, familiar carols play,
  And wild and sweet
  The words repeat
Of peace on earth, good will to men!

I thought how, as the day had come,
The belfries of all Christendom
  Had rolled along
  The unbroken song
Of peace on earth, good will to men!

And in despair I bowed my head:
" There is no peace on earth," I said,
  " For hate is strong
  And mocks the song
Of peace on earth, good will to men! "

Then pealed the bells more loud and deep:
" God is not dead; nor doth he sleep!
  The wrong shall fail,
  The right prevail,
With peace on earth, good will to men! "

(Music available in *The Christmas Carolers' Book*.)

This song appeared December 25, 1863, as a poem entitled " Christmas Bells," written by the beloved American poet, Henry Wadsworth Longfellow, just six months after the Battle of Gettysburg. In it he voiced the anxiety of millions of weary hearts in America during the long dark years of the Civil War.

The author himself had been very closely related to the horror of war, his young son, a lieutenant in the Army of the Potomac, having been seriously wounded in battle. The words "For hate is strong And mocks the song Of peace on earth, good will to men" reflect the atmosphere of those dark days when our forefathers anxiously awaited the dawn of peace between North and South. They contain, however, at the same time those permanent longings of the human heart that continues to pray in every conflict, "O Lord, how long?" and will continue to trust that the right will prevail.

The poem was first published in 1867 and was furnished with a singable, enjoyable melody by J. Baptiste Calkin, a popular London organist, in 1872. The bass notes sound like the ringing of a bell, while the last four measures originated in an old "Amen."

This song will fill the hearts of multitudes with joy so long as church bells ring out the Nativity message at Christmastide.

---

30 *I Saw Three Ships*

(Christmas Day in the Morning)

Traditional   Traditional English
                                             Arr. by Sir John Stainer

I saw three ships come sailing in,
On Christmas Day, on Christmas Day,
I saw three ships come sailing in,
On Christmas Day in the morning.

And what was in those ships all three,
On Christmas Day, on Christmas Day,
And what was in those ships all three,
On Christmas Day in the morning?

The Virgin Mary and Christ were there,
On Christmas Day, on Christmas Day,
The Virgin Mary and Christ were there,
On Christmas Day in the morning.

Pray, whither sailed those ships all three,
  On Christmas Day, on Christmas Day,
Pray, whither sailed those ships all three,
  On Christmas Day in the morning?

O they sailed into Bethlehem,
  On Christmas Day, on Christmas Day,
O they sailed into Bethlehem,
  On Christmas Day in the morning.

And all the bells on earth shall ring,
  On Christmas Day, on Christmas Day,
And all the bells on earth shall ring,
  On Christmas Day in the morning.

And all the angels in heaven shall sing,
  On Christmas Day, on Christmas Day,
And all the angels in heaven shall sing,
  On Christmas Day in the morning.

And all the souls on earth shall sing,
  On Christmas Day, on Christmas Day,
And all the souls on earth shall sing,
  On Christmas Day in the morning.

Then let us all rejoice amain,
  On Christmas Day, on Christmas Day,
Then let us all rejoice amain,
  On Christmas Day in the morning!

This is one of the three best-loved carols of England, partly perhaps because ships play so large a part in the lives of those so close to, and almost surrounded by, the sea. People living in cold, bleak climates have given us carols about pine trees and snow; those in warm countries have given us songs of flowers and birds; and the hill towns relate the stories of shepherds tending their sheep and journeying to the manger. Similarly people living near the water have given us carols about ships carrying precious cargoes.

From England we have this traditional carol, so old that no one knows who wrote either the words or the music. It may well have originated as a folk melody and have been sung by the people as they danced on the village green, for it has a delightful skipping rhythm.

The legend of the Christmas ship is quite common in countries that face the sea. It represents the cargo as Christian love, the Christmas spirit, or as various personages. Sometimes there is more than one ship, as in the case of the song under discussion. The number three may have been suggested by the traditional three Wise Men. In this case the cargo consists of Christ and the Virgin Mary.

That Bethlehem was not a seaport (stanza five) presented no problem to the people of the Middle Ages when this carol arose. They lived in a world of the imagination rather than of fact, and were just as apt to turn Bethlehem into a harbor full of fishermen as some today turn Nazareth or Jerusalem into a contemporary Dutch, English, or French village.

In some versions this song is also known as " Christmas Day in the Morning." One interesting version from Britain included this stanza about Joseph and Mary in the ship:

> O! He did whistle and she did sing,
> And all the bells on earth did ring,
> For joy that our Saviour he was born
> On Christmas Day in the morning.

---

31 It Came Upon the Midnight Clear

Edmund H. Sears, 1850   R. Storrs Willis, 1850

It came upon the midnight clear,
   That glorious song of old,
From angels bending near the earth,
   To touch their harps of gold:
" Peace on the earth, good will to men,
   From heaven's all-gracious King ":
The world in solemn stillness lay,
   To hear the angels sing.

Still through the cloven skies they come,
   With peaceful wings unfurled,
And still their heavenly music floats
   O'er all the weary world:
Above its sad and lowly plains
   They bend on hovering wing,
And ever o'er its Babel sounds
   The blessed angels sing.

O ye, beneath life's crushing load,
   Whose forms are bending low,
Who toil along the climbing way
   With painful steps and slow,
Look now! for glad and golden hours
   Come swiftly on the wing:
O rest beside the weary road,
   And hear the angels sing.

For lo! the days are hastening on,
   By prophet bards foretold,
When with the ever-circling years
   Comes round the age of gold;

When peace shall over all the earth
Its ancient splendors fling,
And the whole world give back the song
Which now the angels sing.

This is one of several carol-hymns of high rank that are of American origin. The author, Edmund Hamilton Sears (1810–1876), was born in the Massachusetts Berkshires, was educated at Union College and the Harvard Divinity School, and spent most of his life as pastor at Wayland, Massachusetts. Several larger churches sought his services, but these offers were declined because of ill-health, frailty of voice, and extreme bashfulness. Though affiliated with the Unitarian Church, he emphasized his Trinitarian faith in the words, " Though I was educated in the Unitarian denomination, I believe and preach the divinity of Christ."

The records indicate that on a cold wintry day in December, 1849, as Dr. Sears sat by the fire in his study and watched the snow coming down, the words of the carol came to him. After completing the stanzas, he sent them to his friend Dr. Morrison, editor of the *Christian Register* in Boston. This editor was so impressed by the poem that he used it at Christmas programs and published it in his magazine. Twenty years later, in 1870, it was printed in the *Hymnal Companion* and in 1871 in *Church Hymns,* both British publications.

Another song we owe to Dr. Sears is not so well known but is praised by Oliver Wendell Holmes as " one of the most beautiful poems ever written " — " Calm on the Listening Ear of Night." He wrote this when only twenty-four years old, in 1834, and revised it in 1851.

The tune " Carol " is an arrangement by Uzziah C. Burnap of Richard Storr Willis' " Study No. 23," made in 1850. Mr. Willis was born in Boston on February 10, 1819, the son of the founder of *The Youth's Companion,* a popular periodical for generations. After having taught German to Yale students, he devoted his energies to editing *The Musical Times* and later *The Musical World.* He died in Detroit, Michigan, May 7, 1900. The quality of this American composer's work is indicated by the fact that Mendelssohn rearranged some of his compositions.

The song became widely used in a short time and will continue its universal appeal. It is one of the first songs, if not the first, that breathes an emphatic social message, expressing the longings of the toiling masses of humanity. The author was writing at a time of extraordinary unrest in the world, for this was the period of the Fugitive Slave Law, the forty-niner gold rush to California, and the Civil War looming over the horizon.

The song speaks equally pointedly today to those who bend "beneath life's crushing load" and to those who long for the time when the "whole world [will] give back the song Which now the angels sing." Its stanzas tell of the multitudes of angels that sang, and of the invitation for weary toilers to rest.

Stanza one is a melodious rendering of the story of the angels and the shepherds.

The second stanza gives assurance that these angels are the very hope of man's constant longing.

Stanza three (seldom printed in our hymnals, therefore given below) portrays the actuality of "woes of sin and strife" and "war with man."

The fourth stanza addresses itself to all who find the burden of life too heavy and refers them from "the weary road" to the angels.

The final stanza reminds us that the song is still valid. Prophets and saints continue to assure us that justice and peace are the ultimate plan of God.

We quote the oft-omitted third stanza:

> Yet with the woes of sin and strife
>   The world has suffered long;
> Beneath the angel-strain have rolled
>   Two thousand years of wrong;
> And man, at war with man, hears not
>   The love song which they bring:
> Oh, hush the noise, ye men of strife,
>   And hear the angels sing.

With so rich a message, it is not surprising that Dr. Morrison who first printed the poem could say that no matter how mediocre he felt his Christmas sermon might have been, the singing of his friend's incomparable hymn more than made up for any deficiencies in his own message.

Scripture passages that are alluded to, more or less specifically, are the following: Isa., chs. 1:18, 19; 2:4; Luke 2:13 f.; Rom. 12:21.

---

32 Joy to the World!

From Psalm 98. Isaac Watts, 1719   George F. Handel, 1742
Arr. by Lowell Mason, 1830

Joy to the world! the Lord is come:
Let earth receive her King;
Let every heart prepare Him room,
And heaven and nature sing,
And heaven and nature sing,
And heaven, and heaven and nature sing.

Joy to the world! the Saviour reigns:
Let men their songs employ;
While fields and floods, rocks, hills, and plains
Repeat the sounding joy,
Repeat the sounding joy,
Repeat, repeat the sounding joy.

No more let sins and sorrow grow,
Nor thorns infest the ground;
He comes to make His blessings flow
Far as the curse is found,
Far as the curse is found,
Far as, far as the curse is found.

He rules the world with truth and grace,
    And makes the nations prove
The glories of His righteousness,
    And wonders of His love,
    And wonders of His love,
    And wonders, and wonders of His love.

Once more we meet an outstanding hymn writer, for Isaac Watts (1674–1748) has justly been called the father of English hymnody, and shares with Charles Wesley the distinction of being the greatest of English hymn writers, leaving some fifty-two published volumes.

He was the son of a Nonconformist boardinghouse keeper, the oldest of nine children, the son of a deacon in Southampton, England, who went to prison twice "for his conscience' sake." The mother carried Isaac in her arms when visiting the father to sing hymns at the prison gate to cheer her husband. When Isaac complained about the listless congregational singing, his father challenged him to provide better hymns. Promptly, at the age of fifteen, the son composed several that were accepted and enjoyed by the congregation.

On his twenty-first birthday he preached his first sermon in the Independent Church in Mark Lane, London. When his health failed in 1708, he offered to resign, but the congregation aided him by engaging an assistant pastor. In 1712 his good friends Sir Thomas and Lady Abney invited him to visit them at their estate, twelve miles away. He accepted, and the intended visit of one week finally became the longest visit recorded, for he remained for thirty-six years, until his death in 1748, preaching in the church whenever he was able. That the relationship in the Abney home was delightful is indicated by the remark made in reply to Mr. Watts's statement about the length of his stay: his gracious hostess declared his visit was the shortest one they had ever experienced!

Watts devoted his energies largely to writing hymns. In 1719, already famous for his *Hymns and Spiritual Songs,* 1707, his collection of paraphrases was printed as *The Psalms of David in the Language of the New Testament.*

The hymn under discussion is a free rendering of a part of Ps. 98, "Make a joyful noise unto the Lord, all the earth: make a loud noise, and rejoice, and sing praise." Watts entitled it "Messiah's Coming and Kingdom." In addition to Ps. 98:4, 6-9 as background, there are also allusions to Gen. 3:17, 18; Rom. 5:20. While it is a song of rejoicing for Israel's salvation from Babylon, the song is concerned with the redemption of the whole world from sin and sorrow, Luke 2:10. See also Isa. 40:3-5 and Phil. 4:4.

So it is a great hymn of the Advent and of the Nativity. He feels all nature thrilling with joy at the Saviour's birth.

It is a forceful expression of missionary zeal and prophetic triumph. "The Saviour reigns" (present tense), even now, although modern missions had not been begun and "religion was never at a lower ebb in England," according to the historian John Richard Green. How powerful and prophetic must have been these words in such a day: "He rules the world with truth and grace, and makes the nations prove . . . His righteousness, and wonders of His love"!

Many hymnals have preserved the text intact except for one word in the original of the first line of the second stanza, "Joy to the earth." A few hymnals have lately omitted the stanza in which the "curse" is mentioned, and the Unitarians change the offending line to "As far as sin is found." One Seventh-Day Adventist book has changed the present tense into the future: "Joy . . . the Lord *will* come," causing the text to center in the Second Coming of Christ. Just to indicate how far groups will lean on others, instead of giving original expression to their own convictions, we quote the text as it appears in *Social Hymns for the Use of Friends of the Rational System of Society,* issued by a group of skeptics in 1838:

> Joy to the world! The light has come,
> The only lawful king:
> Let every heart prepare it room
> And moral nature sing.

The tune "Antioch" is credited by some authorities to an arrangement by Lowell Mason from Handel's *Messiah.* Both facts are questioned in recent years. To many it still seems that the opening phrase resembles the first bar of the chorus "Lift up your heads," and the melody of "and heaven and nature sing" is reminiscent of the introduction to the tenor recitative "Comfort ye my people."

The stanzas may be sung antiphonally to good effect, the congregation singing the first and second lines of each stanza, the choir the third and fourth lines, both joining in the refrain.

---

33   *Lo, How a Rose E'er Blooming*

(A Branch So Fair Has Blossomed)
(Behold, a Branch Is Growing)

German, 15th century   Traditional
Har. by Michael Praetorius, 1609

Lo, how a Rose e'er blooming
    From tender stem hath sprung!
Of Jesse's lineage coming
    As men of old have sung.
It came, a floweret bright,
    Amid the cold of winter,
When half spent was the night.

Isaiah hath foretold it
    In words of promise sure,
And Mary's arms enfold it,
    A virgin meek and pure.
Through God's eternal will
    This Child to her is given,
At midnight calm and still.

The shepherds heard the story
    Proclaimed by angels bright,
How Christ, the Lord of glory
    Was born on earth this night.

To Bethlehem they sped,
  And in the manger found Him,
As angel-heralds said.

This Flower, whose fragrance tender
  With sweetness fills the air,
Dispels with glorious splendor
  The darkness everywhere.
True Man, yet very God,
  From sin and death He saves us
And lightens every load.

O Saviour, Child of Mary,
  Who felt our human woe,
O Saviour, King of glory,
  Who dost our weakness know,
Bring us at length we pray
  To the bright courts of heaven,
And to the endless day.

This carol is widely known in two translations: "Lo, How a Rose E'er Blooming" and "Behold, a Branch Is Growing." This is due to two slightly different German texts, the latter one using the word *Reis* (branch) from Isa. 11:1 f. instead of *Ros'* (rose) of the earlier version. This change seems to have been made fifty-nine years after the first printing of the carol in a Catholic hymnal published in Cologne in 1599. In that early collection the song appeared in twenty-two stanzas.

It is regarded as of fifteenth century German origin. In the complete version of seventeen stanzas, it relates the events of Luke, chs. 1 and 2, and of Matt., ch. 2, with Mary receiving undue attention as compared with her Son who is really the reason for Christmas.

"Praetorius," sometimes called "Görlitz," was arranged by the distinguished German composer Michael Praetorius (1571–1621), who based it on a folk tune that had appeared as early as 1536. The enchanting choral melody did much to popularize the carol, and it has become a favorite in recent years with American *a cappella* choirs.

---

34 *Love Came Down at Christmas*

Hermitage

Christina Rossetti, 1893   R. O. Morris, 1925

Love came down at Christmas,
  Love all lovely, Love divine;
Love was born at Christmas,
  Stars and angels gave the sign.

Worship we the Godhead,
  Love incarnate, Love divine;
Worship we our Jesus:
  But wherewith for sacred sign?

Love shall be our token,
  Love be yours and love be mine,
Love to God and all men,
  Love for plea and gift and sign.

(Music available in *The Hymnal,* Board of Christian Education of the Presbyterian Church in the U.S.A., 1933.)

Christina Rossetti, the author of this charming poem, daughter of an Italian exile, was born in London, December 5, 1830. A High-Church Anglican by conviction, she rejected two suitors on religious grounds. This experience, as well as her austere life, often burdened with poverty, are at times reflected in her early poems. She died in 1894 after two years of great suffering.

The beautiful poem " Love Came Down at Christmas " is characterized by a childlike vividness of devotion and consecrated trust. Since it appeared in her volume *Verses,* published in 1893, it was one of her later, if not last, ones.

The tune "Hermitage" was especially written for *Songs of Praise,* published by the Oxford University Press in 1925, by Reginald Owen Morris, born at York, England, in 1886. After having been educated at Oxford and at the Royal College in London, where he is now on the teaching staff, he was director, from 1926 to 1931, of theory and composition at the Curtis Institute of Music in Philadelphia, Pennsylvania.

The music is of rare beauty with a quiet and somewhat medieval flavor. Because of both the appealing message for children and adults and the attractive music, this song deserves an increasing popularity.

---

35   *Lullay, Thou Little Tiny Child*

(The Coventry Carol)

Robert Croo, d. 1534   English Melody, 1591

Lullay, Thou little tiny Child,
    Bye, bye, lully, lullay;
Lullay, Thou little tiny Child,
    Bye, bye, lully, lullay.

O sisters, too, how may we do,
    For to preserve this day?
This poor Youngling for whom we sing,
    Bye, bye, lully, lullay.

Herod the King, in his raging,
    Charged he hath this day;
His men of might, in his own sight,
    All children young to slay.

Then woe is me, poor Child, for Thee,
    And ever mourn and say;
For Thy parting nor say nor sing,
    Bye, bye, lully, lullay.

(Music available in *The Christmas Carolers' Book* and in
Noëls.)

The poem is drawn from *The Pageant of the Shearmen and the Tailors,* one of the Coventry plays performed by local guilds. It was sponsored by Queen Margaret of England in 1456 and later by Henry VII in 1492. Robert Croo (d. 1534) apparently was the principal author of the pageant in the form in which it has come down to us.

The melody was discovered by Thomas Sharp (1770–1841) as dating from 1591 when the Coventry pageant was again winning public favor. It was published in *A Dissertation on the Pageants, or Dramatic Mysteries, Anciently Performed at Coventry, 1825,* a work that is basic for the early history of the English stage.

---

36 *Now Sing We, Now Rejoice*

(In Dulci Jubilo)

Latin and German, 14th century   Traditional Melody
Arthur Tozer Russell, 1851   Har. by Bartholomew Gesius, 1601

Now sing we, now rejoice,
Now raise to heaven our voice;
    Lo! He from whom joy streameth,
    Poor in the manger lies;
        Yet not so brightly beameth
    The sun in yonder skies!
    Thou my Saviour art!
    Thou my Saviour art!

Given from on high to me,
I cannot rise to Thee:
  O cheer my wearied spirit:
O pure and holy Child,
  Through all Thy grace and merit,
Blest Jesus! Lord most mild,
Draw me after Thee!
Draw me after Thee!

Now through His Son doth shine
The Father's grace divine:
  Death over us hath reigned
Through sin and vanity:
  The Son for us obtained
Eternal joy on high.
May we praise Him there!
May we praise Him there!

O where shall joy be found?
Where but on heavenly ground?
  Where now the angels singing
With all His saints unite,
  Their sweetest praises bringing
In heavenly joy and light:
May we praise Him there!
May we praise Him there!

The Macaronic Version

In dulci jubilo
Now sing with hearts aglow!
  Our delight and pleasure
Lies in praesepio,
  Like sunshine is our treasure

Matris in gremio.
Alpha es et O!
Alpha es et O!

O Jesu, parvule,
For Thee I long alway;
  Comfort my heart's blindness,
O puer optime,
  With all Thy loving-kindness,
O princeps gloriae
Trahe me post te!
Trahe me post te!

While we have treated a paraphrase of this song ("Good Christian Men, Rejoice," No. 22), the traditional elements underlying the rich material have found expression in such varied forms and deserve special further study all the more, since we are thereby introduced to the class of macaronic or mixed hymns.

An old German manuscript of the fourteenth century declares that the original words in "In Dulci Jubilo" were sung to a fourteenth century mystic, Heinrich Suso (1300–1366). This Dominican monk, so the legend relates, was visited by an angel with several companions, and told Suso that God had sent him to bring him happiness. The chief angel took him by the hand and bade him join them in a dance and carol, praising the Christ-child in the words,

In dulci jubilo
Now sing with hearts aglow!

Though legendary, the early reference definitely establishes this as one of the oldest carols that have come to us from Germany.

During the sixteenth century, it was referred to as "An ancient song for Christmas Eve" and was sung widely both in Germany and in Sweden, having been included in several sixteenth century hymnals of Germany and Sweden, including the famous Swedish Lutheran *Piae Cantiones* (Sacred Songs) of 1582. In 1601, a German, Bartholomew Gesius, arranged the melody as we now sing it. Undoubtedly its rhythmic characteristic has contributed much to its survival and even wide popularity.

We have here an excellent example of the so-called " macaronic " or mixed hymns which were common in Germany during the fourteenth and fifteenth centuries. Latin was the language of the church and hence came to be interspersed between lines in the mother tongues of various peoples. (See " Good Christian Men, Rejoice.")

The first English translation was made as early as 1550. The translation we are using appeared in 1851 and is by Arthur Tozer Russell of England.

---

37   O Christmas Tree!

(O Tannenbaum)

German   German Folk Melody
Translator not known

O Christmas Tree! O Christmas Tree!
Thy leaves are so unchanging:
Not only green when summer's here
But also when 'tis cold and drear.
O Christmas Tree! O Christmas Tree!
Thy leaves are so unchanging.

O Christmas Tree! O Christmas Tree!
Much pleasure thou canst give me;
Now often has the Christmas tree
Afforded me the greatest glee!
O Christmas Tree! O Christmas Tree!
Much pleasure thou canst give me.

O Christmas Tree! O Christmas Tree!
How richly God has decked thee!
Thou biddest us true and faithful be

To trust in God unchangingly.
O Christmas Tree! O Christmas Tree!
How richly God has decked thee.

A version with a more religious note:

O Christmas Tree! Fair Christmas Tree!
  A type of life eternal!
O Christmas Tree! Fair Christmas Tree!
  Your boughs are ever vernal.
So fresh and green in summer heat,
And bright when snows lie round your feet.
O Christmas Tree! Fair Christmas Tree!
  A type of life eternal!

O Christmas Tree! Fair Christmas Tree!
  You tell the timeless story.
O Christmas Tree! Fair Christmas Tree!
  You speak of Jesus' glory.
With gifts of love and songs of mirth,
With tidings of our Saviour's birth.
O Christmas Tree! Fair Christmas Tree!
  You tell the timeless story.

O Christmas Tree! Fair Christmas Tree!
  Alight with love and splendor;
O Christmas Tree! Fair Christmas Tree!
  True praise to Christ you render;
In steadfast faith you flash with light,
As stars of God glow through the night.
O Christmas Tree! Fair Christmas Tree!
  Alight with love and splendor.

(Music, English and German texts in *Favorite Christmas,
Folk and Sacred Songs*. The Old Orchard Publishers, Webster
Groves, Mo.)

The decorated evergreen tree is of very early origin, for Virgil already tells us of the magical fairy tree with its swinging toys. At the Roman festivals called Saturnalia, it was customary to have trees laden with decorations and gifts. During the barbarian invasions the Goths adopted the custom of the Saturnalia, including that of the tree, and so brought it into Germany.

The tree did not become a part of the Christian Christmas festival until early in the sixteenth century. A popular tale credits Martin Luther with introducing it into the home. While he was walking home on Christmas Eve over the snow-covered ground, he was impressed by the stars shining through the fir trees to the point of being reminded of the first Christmas Eve. So he cut down a small fir tree and decorated it with candles. From Luther's home the custom spread into other homes in Germany, then into the churches and into other countries, until now even tropical countries frequently make adaptations to serve as decorated trees, using also cactus, palms, and other varieties.

The first decorated Christmas tree in England was introduced by Prince Albert, German-born husband of Queen Victoria. Community trees throughout the United States, from the National Christmas Tree in Washington, D.C., lighted by the President on Christmas Eve, to the Nation's Christmas Tree in General Grant National Park, California, where services are held on Christmas Day, bring pleasure and inspiration to young and old, rich and poor alike.

"O Christmas Tree" ("O Tannenbaum") is the most popular carol about the Christmas tree and is rivaled only by the lovely "Silent Night" in popular favor in Germany.

The melody is an old folk tune of the Middle Ages. It is familiar now also as that of Maryland's state song ("Maryland, My Maryland") which was one of the most popular Confederate songs of the Civil War. Several other state songs and numerous college songs have likewise adopted the tune.

---

38 O Come, All Ye Faithful

(Adeste Fideles)
(Come Hither, Ye Faithful)

Latin hymn, 18th century   Wade's *Cantus Diversi*, 1751
Tr. Frederick Oakeley, 1841

O come, all ye faithful,
Joyfully triumphant,
O come ye, O come ye to Bethlehem!
Come and behold Him,
Born the King of angels!
  O come, let us adore Him,
  O come, let us adore Him,
  O come, let us adore Him,
  Christ the Lord!

The brightness of glory,
Light of light eternal,
Our lowly nature He hath not abhorred:
Son of the Father,
Word of God incarnate!

O sing, choirs of angels,
Sing in exultation!
Through heaven's high arches be your praises poured!
Now to our God be
Glory in the highest!

Amen! Lord, we bless Thee,
Born for our salvation,
O Jesus, forever be Thy name adored;
Word of the Father,
Now in flesh appearing!

(Music available, also the Latin text, in *Carols, Customs and Costumes Around the World*. The Old Orchard Publishers, Webster Groves, Mo.)

Recent research has given us clarity as to the origin of both text and tune of this very popular Christmas song. In 1946 an English vicar discovered a small manuscript of musical selections for chapel use among Roman Catholics which leads us to more certain and more definite conclusions.

Whereas before this discovery some researchers speculated that the hymn was to be ascribed to Bonaventura, and others came to the vague conclusion that it came from Germany or France in the seventeenth or eighteenth century, it now seems clear that the author was John Francis Wade, a man whose task it was to copy music for Catholic institutions and families in various places. He was an Englishman by birth but had moved to Douai in France. There he wrote the hymn in 1744 and set it to the music with which it is still most frequently used.

An edition of Wade's manuscript *Cantus Diversi pro Dominicis et Festis per Annum* appeared in 1750 for the English Roman Catholic College in Lisbon, Portugal. Since it was also used in the chapel of the Portuguese Embassy in London, the music received the name "Portuguese Hymn," though it is most frequently referred to as "Adeste Fideles," the first two words of the Latin version.

While the original Latin text had eight stanzas, only two or three are used generally. Its tremendous popularity, having been translated into more than one hundred and twenty-five languages, is due to both its majestic melody and its exalted message, the incarnation. God has appeared in the form of man and has revealed the love of the Father's heart. The way of reconciliation to God has been opened, men's fears have been quieted, and choirs of angels sing the triumph songs.

The imagery is so vivid and simple that a child can understand it and enter meaningfully into the experience of worship and joy.

The translation in most common use is by Frederick Oakeley (1802–1880). Canon Oakeley was educated at Christ Church, Oxford, winning special honors in Latin.

Oft-omitted stanzas:

> See how the shepherds,
> Summoned to His cradle,
> Leaving their flocks, draw nigh with lowly fear;

We too will thither
Bend our joyful footsteps.

Lo, star-led chieftains,
Magi, Christ adoring,
Offer Him incense, gold, and myrrh;
We to the Christ-child
Bring our hearts' oblations.

Child, for us sinners,
Poor and in a manger,
Fain would we embrace Thee, with awe and love;
Who would not love Thee,
Loving us so dearly?

---

39 *O Come, O Come, Emmanuel*

From Latin, 12th century
Tr. mainly by John Mason Neale, 1851

Ancient plain song,
13th century

O come, O come, Emmanuel,
And ransom captive Israel,
That mourns in lonely exile here
Until the Son of God appear.
Rejoice! Rejoice! Emmanuel
Shall come to thee, O Israel!

O come, Thou Rod of Jesse's stem,
From every foe deliver them
That trust Thy mighty power to save,
And give them victory o'er the grave.

O come, Thou Dayspring from on high,
And cheer us by Thy drawing nigh;
Disperse the gloomy clouds of night,
And death's dark shadows put to flight.

O come, Thou Key of David, come,
And open wide our heavenly home;
Make safe the way that leads on high,
And close the path to misery.

O come, O come, Thou Lord of might,
Who to Thy tribes on Sinai's height
In ancient times didst give the law,
In cloud, and majesty, and awe.

O come, Desire of nations, bind
All peoples in one heart and mind;
Bid envy, strife, and discord cease;
Fill the whole world with heaven's peace.

This hymn comes from the Latin, being a translation of the seven greater antiphons (short anthem verses) that were sung in the Roman Church at vespers on the seven days before Christmas during the ninth century or earlier. The word "antiphon" suggests that the lines were sung alternately either before or after the Magnificat by two choirs sitting opposite each other in the chancel. Here are the opening lines of the seven, also called "Great O's," with a translation of the key words:

1. O Sapientia, quae ex ore altissimi. "Wisdom."
2. O Adonai et Dux domus Israel. "Lord."
3. O Radix Jesse, qui stas in signum. "Root of Jesse."
4. O Clavis David et sceptrum domus. "Key of David."
5. O Oriens, splendor lucis aeternae. "Orient" (East).
6. O Rex gentium et desideratus. "King."
7. O Emmanuel, Rex et legifer. "Emmanuel" (God with us).

Sometime in the twelfth century, according to Neale, or in the thirteenth century, according to Percy Dearmer (English hymnodist), or in the eighteenth century, according to the Julian Dictionary, someone recast five of these antiphons, changed their order, and added the refrain. Dr. John Mason Neale (1818–1866) translated these five "Great O's" which had been set into metrical Latin. Dr. Neale was a Cambridge scholar and renowned hymnologist to whom we owe the well-known songs "Jerusalem the Golden," "Christian, Dost Thou See Them," "The Day of Resurrection," "Come Ye Faithful, Raise the Strain," and "Art Thou Weary, Art Thou Languid," to name only a few of the better-known of his many contributions to hymnody.

Henry Sloane Coffin, to whom we owe the alteration of the sixth stanza quoted above, is best known as having served as pastor of Madison Avenue Presbyterian Church, New York City, and as President of Union Theological Seminary in that city. He was born in New York, January 5, 1877.

The spirit of the hymn under discussion is medieval in thought and imagery but serves equally well today to bring to us the message of the Advent season. Whereas the emphasis originally had been on death and judgment, this hymn reflects the new note of rejoicing introduced by the antiphons.

It is helpful to see briefly the Scriptural basis of these antiphons, following the order of their appearance in the verses quoted above:

Stanza one — "Emmanuel" (Immanuel, Emanuel, varied forms) means "God with us," and appears in Isa. 7:14 and 8:8, as also in Matt. 1:23. To Christians the expression refers to Christ who will ransom his Church (the spiritual Israel) from exile.

Stanza two — "The Rod [or Branch] of Jesse" alludes to Isa. 11:1, where the Redeemer is described.

Stanza three — "The Dayspring" is mentioned in Luke 1:78.

Stanza four — "The Key of David" appears in Rev. 3:7, referring to the Christ who opens doors that lead to God and to life eternal.

Stanza five — The Lord (*Adonai* in Hebrew), too sacred for the Jews to pronounce, is proclaimed to Israel at Mount Sinai, where the Law was given midst lightning and thunder (Ex., ch. 19).

Stanza six — "The Desire of nations" alludes to Hag. 2:7 (implied in Mal. 3:1). Along with the note of judgment, "And I will shake all nations," there is the note of promise, "The Desire of all nations shall come: and I will fill this house with glory, saith the Lord of hosts."

The refrain is an echo of Zech. 9:9, introducing the note of joy and thus making this hymn a stately song of gladness because the Promised One is coming.

The tune "Veni Emmanuel" is written in the first Gregorian mode. The harmony is largely in the normal minor mode, giving it a unique appeal. When used in the Christmas season, you will hear it echo and re-echo for days and weeks.

While it can be sung throughout in unison, it lends itself well also to men's voices singing the stanzas and all voices in harmony joining in the refrain. Interesting effects can also be produced through antiphonal renditions.

---

40   O Holy Night!

(Cantique de Noël)

M. Cappeau de Roquemaure   Adolphe Adam, 1803–1856
Tr. by John S. Dwight, 1813–1893

O holy night! the stars are brightly shining,
    It is the night of the dear Saviour's birth;
Long lay the world in sin and error pining,
    Till He appeared and the soul felt its worth.
A thrill of hope, the weary soul rejoices,
    For yonder breaks a new and glorious morn.
Fall on your knees, O hear the angel voices!
    O night divine, O night when Christ was born!
    O night, O holy night, O night divine!

Led by the light of faith serenely beaming,
    With glowing hearts by His cradle we stand;
So led by light of a star sweetly gleaming,
    Here came the Wise Men from the Orient land.
The King of Kings lay thus in lowly manger,
    In all our trials born to be our friend;
He knows our need, to our weakness is no stranger,

Behold your King, before Him lowly bend!
Behold your King, before Him lowly bend!

Truly He taught us to love one another;
His law is love and His gospel is peace;
Chains shall He break, for the slave is our brother,
And in His name all oppression shall cease.
Sweet hymns of joy in grateful chorus raise we,
Let all within us praise His holy name!
Christ is the Lord! O praise His name forever!
His power and glory evermore proclaim!
His power and glory evermore proclaim!

While it is impossible to have complete and final statistics as to Christmas songs, it is frequently claimed that France has the largest number of carols to its credit. Furthermore, there are differences of opinion as to the classification of songs into carols and hymns. It is one of the glories of Christmas music that it varies all the way from the simplest carol of folk song origin to the great oratorios by the masters of music. While we frequently have to look into the distant past for information and then conclude that both words and tune are traditional, the song before us takes us back approximately a century only. There we find a melody and an accompaniment by Adolphe Adam (1803–1856) that blends so perfectly with the words that it could well be an integral composition.

However, we owe our English translation to John S. Dwight (1813–1893), cofounder of the Harvard Musical Association and editor of *Dwight's Journal of Music,* who translated " Cantique de Noël," the original French words by M. Cappeau de Roquemaure. Unfortunately, here again information concerning his life is not available. But we can say that his very opening words, " O holy night," awaken a feeling of reverence and the scene is set for us by the succeeding words, " the stars are brightly shining." The music weaves the atmosphere for the lyrics so beautifully as to be almost enchanting.

Adolphe Adam, the composer, was born in Paris in 1803. His father, a professor at the Paris Conservatory (1797–1842), after first insisting that his son study law, later allowed him to enter the conservatory. His comic operas and light ballets achieved such success that his reputation extended to London, Berlin, and St. Petersburg. France will long remember him as its popular music critic and composer, but the world will know him better for his " Cantique de Noël." There was a time when people flocked to Paris at Christmas time to hear his most popular composition presented in the larger churches of the city. Today the song is heard in almost every community where Christmas is known and observed.

We are told that, on Christmas Eve in 1870, during the Franco-Prussian War, when Paris was besieged, the French and Germans faced each other in trenches before the city. Suddenly a young Frenchman jumped out of his trench, and in a beautiful singing voice astonished the Germans with Adolphe Adam's incomparable " Cantique de Noël." The men on the opposite side seemed awe-struck and not a shot was fired in his direction. When the French singer had finished the carol, a tall German responded. He came out of his trench to sing in his own language Luther's noted Christmas hymn, " From Heaven Above to Earth I Come."

---

41 O Little Town of Bethlehem

Bishop Phillips Brooks, 1868   Lewis H. Redner, 1868

O little town of Bethlehem,
   How still we see thee lie;
Above thy deep and dreamless sleep
   The silent stars go by.
Yet in thy dark streets shineth
   The everlasting Light;
The hopes and fears of all the years
   Are met in thee tonight.

For Christ is born of Mary;
  And gathered all above,
While mortals sleep, the angels keep
  Their watch of wondering love.
O morning stars, together
  Proclaim the holy birth;
And praises sing to God the King,
  And peace to men on earth!

How silently, how silently
  The wondrous gift is given!
So God imparts to human hearts
  The blessings of His heaven.
No ear may hear His coming,
  But in this world of sin,
Where meek souls will receive Him, still
  The dear Christ enters in.

O holy Child of Bethlehem!
  Descend to us, we pray;
Cast out our sin, and enter in,
  Be born in us today.
We hear the Christmas angels
  The great glad tidings tell;
O come to us, abide with us,
  Our Lord Emmanuel!

Phillips Brooks was born in Boston, December 13, 1835. He was
blessed with parents noted for their educational and religious in-
terests. After graduating from Harvard he tried teaching in the
Boston Latin School but concluded, "I have failed most signally in
teaching school but I am not quite ready to acknowledge myself
wholly unequal to all this wide world's work." Thereupon he entered
the Episcopal Theological Seminary at Alexandria, Virginia, and was

ordained to the ministry in 1859. After serving for ten years in the Church of the Advent and Holy Trinity Church in Philadelphia, he was called to Trinity Church, Boston. On October 14, 1891, he was consecrated bishop, but lived less than two years to enjoy this honor — until January 23, 1893.

While noted as the " prince among preachers " of his day, having been gifted in powerful speech (1,250 words a minute, we are told!), rich in metaphor, he is most affectionately remembered because of the popular verses of " O Little Town of Bethlehem."

In 1865 he spent a year in the Holy Land and on the day before Christmas he went on horseback from Jerusalem to Bethlehem and visited the fields where, traditionally, the shepherds watched their flocks. From ten o'clock in the evening until three the next morning, he attended the Christmas service in the Church of the Nativity. This sublime experience and cherished memory became the background three years later, when he was but thirty-two years old, for this carol written for the children of his Sunday school in Holy Trinity Church, Philadelphia. He had written the children from Palestine, " I remember especially on Christmas Eve when I was standing in the old church in Bethlehem, close to the spot where Jesus was born, when the whole church was ringing hour after hour with the splendid hymns of praise to God, how again and again it seemed as if I could hear voices I know well, telling each other of the 'Wonderful Night' of the Saviour's birth, as I had heard them a year before."

A very brief analysis of the carol follows.

Stanza one — Bethlehem is still, asleep, dark in 1865, before the era of street lights. But the "everlasting Light" (John 1:9; 8:12) came that holy night in answer to the "hopes and fears" as to poverty, misery, and war.

Stanza two — Here we have the Scripture narrative in verse form. The wondering angels keep watch (Luke, ch. 2); the "morning stars" burst forth in song (Job 38:7).

Stanza three — As Christ was born in the silent watches of the night, so he enters human hearts today in silence, when they are opened to him.

Stanza four — A prayer that the Christ-child "be born in us" and fill our hearts with love. While written for children, understood and loved by them, the carol is equally popular with adults and rightly so.

Another stanza, the third in the original version, is seldom printed in hymnals but is equally appealing:

> Where children, pure and happy,
>> Pray to the blessed Child;
> Where misery cries out to Thee,
>> Son of the Mother mild;
> Where charity stands watching,
>> And faith holds wide the door,
> The dark night wakes, the glory breaks
>> And Christmas comes once more.

The carol tune was written by Lewis Redner, organist and Sunday school superintendent at Holy Trinity Church and a successful businessman dealing in real estate. He was born in Philadelphia in 1831 and died in Atlantic City in 1908. He had been requested by Phillips Brooks to compose a melody and had promised the children to have it for a certain Sunday. At bedtime the following Saturday the melody was still unwritten. During the night he was suddenly awakened by an " angel strain " ringing in his ears. He jotted down the melody and filled in the harmony the next morning. Redner always insisted it was a gift from heaven.

When the tune was to be named, Redner suggested, " We will call it ' St. Phillips.' " Dr. Brooks replied, " You must write the music and we will call it ' St. Louis ' " — a generous gesture by the bighearted rector. The words and tune, printed on leaflets, were sung by six teachers and thirty-six Sunday school children. Though published in *The Church Porch* in 1874, the song was practically forgotten until 1892 when it appeared in the hymnal of the Episcopal Church. Since then it ranks high in popularity in both the United States and England.

At times, especially in England, it is sung to the tune " Forest Green," associated familiarly with " Thy Word Is like a Garden, Lord."

42 *Once in Royal David's City*

Cecil F. Alexander, 1848   Henry J. Gauntlett, 1849

Once in royal David's city
  Stood a lowly cattle shed,
Where a mother laid her Baby
  In a manger for His bed:
Mary was that mother mild,
Jesus Christ, her little Child.

He came down to earth from heaven
  Who is God and Lord of all,
And His shelter was a stable,
  And His cradle was a stall:
With the poor, and mean, and lowly,
Lived on earth our Saviour holy.

And, through all His wondrous childhood,
  He would honor and obey,
Love, and watch the lowly maiden
  In whose gentle arms He lay;
Christian children all must be
Mild, obedient, good as He.

For He is our childhood's pattern;
  Day by day like us He grew;
He was little, weak, and helpless,
  Tears and smiles like us He knew;
And He feeleth for our sadness,
And He shareth in our gladness.

And our eyes at last shall see Him,
  Through His own redeeming love;
For that Child so dear and gentle

Is our Lord in heaven above,
And He leads His children on
To the place where He is gone.

Not in that poor lowly stable,
 With the oxen standing by,
We shall see Him; but in heaven,
 Set at God's right hand on high;
When like stars His children crowned,
All in white shall wait around.

This beautiful Christmas hymn was written by Cecil Frances Alexander, who was born in Dublin, Ireland, in 1823, and died in 1895. In 1850 she married Rev. William Alexander, who became archbishop of Armagh and primate of all Ireland.

Of her hymns, some four hundred in all, including the favorites "There Is a Green Hill Far Away," and "Jesus Calls Us: O'er the Tumult," this one is most beloved and appreciated by children.

One authority stated that she wrote it for her godchildren when they "complained that their Bible lessons were dreary." It interprets the words in the Apostles' Creed, "I believe . . . in Jesus Christ . . . our Lord; who was . . . born of the Virgin Mary." She succeeded in telling the story so simply that the hymn has become a favorite children's hymn, even in seasons other than Christmas. How could it be otherwise with such appealing simplicity?

For He is our childhood's pattern;
 Day by day like us He grew;
He was little, weak, and helpless,
 Tears and smiles like us He knew;
And He feeleth for our sadness,
And He shareth in our gladness.

The song was published in 1848 in *Hymns for Little Children,* a collection that went through more than one hundred editions in England.

Stanza one is a metrical version of the details from Luke 2:4, 7.

Stanza two adds pictorial details of the Nativity.

Stanza three paraphrases the statement of Luke 2:51, 52.

Stanza four refers to Jesus as the ideal for every child, Luke 2:40.

Stanza five expresses the Creed's articles, "the resurrection of the body" and "the life everlasting." Cf. I Cor. 2:9; Rev. 1:7.

Stanza six presents the picture of heaven reflected in the book of Revelation. The stars in line five allude to Dan. 12:3; the white garments, to Rev. 7:9-17.

The melody was written by Henry J. Gauntlett, organist at his father's church in Olney, England, at the age of nine. At fifteen he presented a creditable performance of Handel's *Messiah*. Mendelssohn praised him highly for his knowledge of the history of music, of acoustical laws, as well as practical experience. He edited many hymnals and wrote thousands of tunes.

The hymn should not be sung too fast lest the many fast-moving notes be slurred over.

----

43 O Thou Joyful Day

(O Sanctissima)

Traditional German   Sicilian Mariners' Hymn, 1794

O thou joyful day,
O thou blessed day,
   Holy, peaceful Christmastide!
Earth's hopes awaken,
Christ life has taken,
   Laud Him, O laud Him on every side!

O thou joyful day,
O thou blessed day,
   Holy, peaceful Christmastide!
Christ's light is beaming
Our souls redeeming,
   Laud Him, O laud Him on every side!

O thou joyful day,
O thou blessed day,
   Holy, peaceful Christmastide!
King of all glory,
We bow before Thee,
   Laud Him, O laud Him on every side!

(Music, English and German texts in *Favorite Christmas,
Folk and Sacred Songs*. The Old Orchard Publishers, Webster
Groves, Mo.)

Not many convincing facts about the origin of this poem (as much
a hymn as a carol) are known. It is based on "O Sanctissima"
and has come down to us as the "Sicilian Mariners' Hymn."

It received its original title from the first line of the Latin text,
composed and dedicated to the Virgin Mary, as seen in the form in
which it appeared about 1794 in connection with Tattersall's musical
edition of Merrick's *Psalms*.

O Sanctissima,
O Piissima
Dulcis Virgo Maria,
Mater amata,
Intemerata,
Ora, ora pro nobis.

O most holy one,
O most lowly one,
Dearest Virgin, Maria,
Mother of fair love,
Home of the Spirit Dove,
Ora, ora pro nobis.

Help us in sadness drear,
Port of gladness near,
Virgin Mother, Maria,

In pity heeding,
Hear thou our pleading,
Ora, ora pro nobis.

Some researchers mention southern France as one of the possible sources for the tune. Even today, on St. Mary's Day, the gondoliers in Venice sing this hymn as they row their gondolas through the city of canals, the "Bride of the Sea."

We are on more solid ground, figuratively and literally, when we say that in 1816 Johannes Falk wrote for this melody a "tri-holiday" song, with three texts for the three main festivals of the Church year — Christmas, Easter, and Pentecost — for the use of the orphan children under his care at Weimar, each one beginning with a variation of the first two lines of the stanza as indicated below:

O thou joyous day,
O thou holy day —

followed by the line that referred to the particular season:

Grace-revealing Christmastide!
Grace-revealing Eastertide!
Grace-revealing Whitsuntide!

Later an unknown writer added two more stanzas for each festival, and still later a fourth was added to the Christmas version.

Even today this hymn, particularly the Christmas text, ranks high among the favorite ones in Germany.

The tune is varyingly known as "Sicily," "Sicilian Mariners," "Mariner," and "O Sanctissima."

In World War I, in the Argonne Forest, when German troops in their trenches sang "O Du Froehliche!", the German version of the song under discussion, we are told the French answered with their own carol, "Noël! Noël!" Thereupon the men exchanged gifts of chocolate and other small presents. To honor Christmas Day, guns on both sides were silent for several hours.

44   Rise Up, Shepherd, an' Foller

Negro Spiritual   Arr. by Prof. R. J. Stanovsky, 1936

Dere's a star in de eas' on Christmas morn,
Rise up, shepherd, an' foller;
It'll lead to de place where de Saviour's born,
Rise up, shepherd, an' foller.

Leave yo' ewes an' leave yo' lambs,
Rise up, shepherd, an' foller.
Leave yo' sheep an' leave yo' rams,
Rise up, shepherd, an' foller.

Foller, foller,
Rise up, shepherd, an' foller.
Foller, foller,
Rise up, shepherd, an' foller.
Foller de star o' Bethlehem,
Rise up, shepherd, an' foller.

(Music in four parts available in *Carols, Customs and Costumes Around the World.* The Old Orchard Publishers, Webster Groves, Mo.)

This carol is typically Negro in its short sentences and in its simplicity. It might well be classified as a shepherd carol, since the shepherd is central throughout.

As has happened not only in Negro spirituals but in carols of various countries, the details of the Nativity story are not always presented accurately. In this case we have the star in the east on Christmas morn, not even on Twelfth-night! We have shepherds following the star, not Wise Men.

The second stanza is much more faithful to the narrative. The following is another version of it:

If ye' take good heed to de angel's words,
Rise up, shepherd, an' foller,
Yo'll forget yo' flocks, yo'll forget yo' herds;
Rise up, shepherd, an' foller.

---

45 *Shepherds! Shake Off Your Drowsy Sleep*

Traditional

French
Arr. by Sir John Stainer

Shepherds! shake off your drowsy sleep,
Rise and leave your silly sheep;
Angels from heaven around loud singing,
Tidings of great joy are bringing.
Shepherds! the chorus come and swell!
Sing Noël, O sing Noël!

Hark, even now, the bells ring round,
Listen to their merry sound;
Hark! how the birds new songs are making,
As if winter's chains were breaking.

See how the flowers all burst anew,
Thinking snow is summer dew;
See how the stars afresh are glowing,
All their brightest beams bestowing.

Cometh at length the age of peace,
Strife and sorrow now shall cease;
Prophets foretold the wondrous story
Of this heaven-born Prince of Glory.

Shepherds! then up and quick away,
Seek the Babe ere break of day;
He is the hope of every nation,
All in Him shall find salvation.

This beautiful old carol comes to us from the Besançon country, in France, very near the mountains of Switzerland. On the hillsides shepherds tended their sheep in all kinds of weather.

While reflecting in considerable detail the story of the Nativity in Luke, ch. 2, there are also several more modern touches as well as the medieval mystery play influences to be observed. The bells ring round, the birds make new sounds, the flowers burst all anew, the age of peace when strife and sorrow shall cease is awaited. Therefore the call to seek the Babe and find in him salvation.

The mystery plays given in the churches portrayed the Christmas star in the heavens and the shepherds watching their sheep. In one of the plays the shepherds hurried off through the night to the manger bringing their gifts of a brooch with a bell attached, and a horn spoon large enough to hold forty peas! In another play one shepherd offered his hat as a gift and another presented his mittens to the Christchild to keep His hands warm.

While we do not know who wrote the words or the melody, it is clear that we owe the beautiful arrangement to Sir John Stainer, the beloved English organist and composer. For more facts concerning him, see " What Child Is This? "

———

46 *Silent Night! Holy Night!*

Tr. from Joseph Mohr, 1818   Franz Gruber, 1818

Silent night! holy night!
All is calm, all is bright;
Round yon Virgin Mother and Child,
Holy Infant so tender and mild:
Sleep in heavenly peace,
Sleep in heavenly peace.

Silent night! holy night!
Darkness flies, all is light;
Shepherds hear the angels sing:

Alleluia! hail the King!
Christ the Saviour is born,
Christ the Saviour is born.

Silent night! holy night!
Guiding Star, lend thy light!
See the Eastern Wise Men bring
Gifts and homage to our King!
Christ the Saviour is born,
Christ the Saviour is born.

Silent night! holy night!
Wondrous Star, lend thy light!
With the angels let us sing
Alleluia to our King!
Christ the Saviour is born,
Christ the Saviour is born.

(German, Japanese, and Spanish versions with music are
available in *Carols, Customs and Costumes Around the World.*
The Old Orchard Publishers, Webster Groves, Mo.)

Now we come to the best-loved and most widely used of all
Christmas carols. "Silent Night" has been translated into no
less than ninety languages and dialects.

It was written December 24, 1818, by Joseph Mohr (1792–1848),
assistant Catholic priest in an obscure village, Oberndorf, near Salzburg, Austria. As happens frequently with matters that rapidly achieve
world-wide fame, legends gathered around the origin of this song
and we are compelled to critically choose between fancy and fact.

One fanciful attempt to explain the origin of the song relates that
at a Christmas celebration in the schoolhouse, Mohr withdrew for a
time and then returned with a folded sheet of paper on which he had
rapidly written the carol. Another report states that Mohr had attended a crude dramatization of the Christmas story which stirred
him so deeply that on his way home he climbed a small mountain

and let the night speak to him, with the result that he went home
at midnight and composed the noted hymn.

One of the reasons for the universal appeal of this hymn is the
fact that it so beautifully and progressively portrays the Nativity
story. First there is the quiet darkness with the one light penetrating
it. Then there comes the sudden flood of glory-light, the shepherds,
the messenger and with him the heavenly host with their " Gloria."
Then the strange kingly figures bring not merely gifts but " homage,"
genuine devotion. The climax is revealed in the prayer that we may
join the angel choir in praise of the Saviour and King.

In 1937, Dr. Max Gehmacher, a relative of Franz Gruber who composed the melody, published in German *The Christmas Carol, How
It Came Into Existence and What It Really Is*. He relates that when
the organ failed to function on December 24, 1818, Father Mohr de-
cided to write a new hymn as a substitute for the organ music that
night, hoping that Franz Gruber (1787–1863), the organist and
teacher of the village school, would be able to set it to music. It was
written for two voices and guitar. Mohr sang the tenor lead, Gruber
sang bass and played the guitar, and according to some authorities,
a choir of girls from the village joined in the melody.

The hymn and tune became immensely popular in Germany and
Austria through their use by wandering Tyrolese singers. The organ
builder from the Zillerthal was so impressed by the song that upon
his return home he introduced it to the Strasser sisters, who added it
to their repertoire of mountain songs, calling it " The Song from
Heaven." When, by 1854, the song had mistakenly been regarded as
a folk song or a composition by Michael Haydn, an inquiry was sent
to Salzburg (by the court musicians in Berlin) asking if the manuscript of " Silent Night " by Michael Haydn might be in St. Peter's
Church. As it happened, Felix Gruber, youngest son of Franz Gruber,
was serving as a choirboy in St. Peter's and the request quite naturally
was brought to his attention. When the question was finally presented
to Franz Gruber, the following signed statement was issued by him:

" Authentic Occasion for the Writing of the Christmas Song
' Silent Night, Holy Night.'

" It was on December 24 of the year 1818 when Joseph Mohr,

then assistant pastor of the newly established St. Nicholas' parish church in Oberndorf, handed to Franz Gruber, who was attending to the duties of organist (and was at the same time a schoolmaster in Arnsdorf) a poem, with the request that he write for it a suitable melody arranged for two solo voices, chorus, and a guitar accompaniment. On that very same evening the latter, in fulfillment of this request made to him as a music expert, handed to the pastor his simple composition, which was thereupon immediately performed on that holy night of Christmas Eve and received with all acclaim. As this Christmas song has come into the Tyrol through the well-known Zillerthaler, and since it has also appeared in a somewhat altered form in a collection of songs in Leipzig, the composer has the honor to dare to place beside it the original.

" Franz Gruber

" Town Parish Choir Director and Organist, Hallein, December 30, 1854."

The King of Prussia, Frederick William IV, heard " Silent Night " for the first time in 1854 when it was sung by the entire choir of the Imperial Church in Berlin. He declared that this song should be given first place in all Christmas concerts in his country.

In 1838 it had appeared in the *Leipziger Gesangbuch,* in 1840 in a *Catholic Hymn and Prayer Book.* By 1849 it had started its journey around the world by being included in a Methodist compilation in the United States, *Devotional Harmony* — only in a very free paraphrase, however.

The translator of the well-nigh perfect translation that is in general use now unfortunately remains unknown.

In addition to being more widely used than any other Christmas carol, including broadcasts each Christmas Eve from Hallein, Gruber's later home, and the annual rendition by the late beloved Schumann-Heink, the carol has been the subject of numerous articles, pamphlets, stories, novels, plays, and even a movie.

William C. Gannett, 1840–1923   Adam Geibel, 1855–1933

Sleep, my little Jesus,
  On Thy bed of hay,
While the shepherds homeward
  Journey on their way.
Mother is Thy shepherd
  And will her vigil keep:
Did the voices wake Thee?
  O sleep, my Jesus, sleep!
    Softly sleep, sweetly sleep,
    My Jesus, sleep!

Sleep, my little Jesus,
  While Thou art my own!
Ox and ass Thy neighbors,
  Shalt Thou have a throne?
Will they call me blessed?
  Shall I stand and weep?
Be it far, Jehovah!
  O sleep, my Jesus, sleep!

Sleep, my little Jesus,
  Wonder-baby mine!
Well the singing angels
  Greet Thee as divine.
Through my heart, as heaven,
  Low the echoes sweep
Of glory to Jehovah!
  O sleep, my Jesus, sleep!

(Music available in *Music Supplement of the World's Great Madonnas,* by Maus. Harper & Brothers.)

In "Sleep, My Little Jesus" we have another beautiful Christmas lullaby. The words were written by William C. Gannett (1840–1923), a Unitarian minister in Rochester, New York. While he was an industrious writer, he may well be remembered chiefly by this charming little poem.

The enchanting melody was written by the noted blind musician Adam Geibel. Born in Baden, Germany, September 15, 1855, he came to Philadelphia at the age of seven where he rendered a noble service as organist, choirmaster, composer, and publisher. He was a striking example of the contribution the blind have made to music.

Though born a normal child, at the age of eight or nine he developed an eye infection. Having been treated with medicine that was too strong, he lost his sight completely. Undismayed, he bravely went ahead and even claimed that he did not regret his loss, for it enabled him to develop his God-given talent in music.

He had a special reputation as a writer in four parts for men's voices. Included in his most successful quartets was the well-known "Kentucky Babe." His aim was to write for the larger body of people who could enjoy and appreciate the simpler type of music.

For many years he was organist at the Stetson Mission. He died August 3, 1933, in Philadelphia, which had been his home during all his active years.

The lullaby lends itself well to four-part singing, but added beauty is achieved by singing the refrain in unison.

---

48 There's a Song in the Air!

Josiah G. Holland, 1819–1881   Karl P. Harrington
                                                      1861–1929

There's a song in the air!
There's a star in the sky!
There's a mother's deep prayer
And a baby's low cry!
And the star rains its fire

While the beautiful sing,
For the manger of Bethlehem
    Cradles a King!

There's a tumult of joy
    O'er the wonderful birth,
For the Virgin's sweet boy
    Is the Lord of the earth.
Ay! the star rains its fire
    While the beautiful sing,
For the manger of Bethlehem
    Cradles a King!

In the light of that star
    Lie the ages impearled;
And that song from afar
    Has swept over the world.
Every hearth is aflame,
    And the beautiful sing
In the homes of the nations
    That Jesus is King!

We rejoice in the light,
    And we echo the song
That comes down through the night
    From the heavenly throng.
Ay! we shout to the lovely
    Evangel they bring,
And we greet in His cradle
    Our Saviour and King!

(Music available in *The Methodist Hymnal* and others.)

The author of this relatively recent carol, first published in 1879, was the eminent American editor, Josiah Gilbert Holland. He was born in Belchertown, Massachusetts, July 24, 1819. He attended Northampton High School but had to withdraw because of ill-health. His life is an excellent example of success through perseverance. For a time he taught school, carried on a business in photography, and conducted a writing school. At twenty-one he studied medicine, graduating from Berkshire Medical College.

Successively he abandoned the medical practice and teaching and established a weekly paper which lived six months! Then came a turn for the better. In 1850 he became associated with the editorship of the *Republican,* Springfield, Massachusetts, where he became famous through his *Timothy Titcomb's Letters,* characterized by humor and common sense. When he was in Europe during the years 1868–1869, he met Roswell Smith, and upon their return the two joined Charles Scribner in founding *Scribner's Monthly,* of which Holland was the editor until his death, October 12, 1881.

The carol beautifully reflects not only the Nativity events of the star, the mother, and the manger; but it indicates that the " song from afar has swept over the world," so that Jesus is King in the homes of the nations as " we greet in His cradle our Saviour and King." The song was first published in Holland's *Complete Poetical Writings* in 1879 and won immediate favor, especially with Sunday school members.

When published in *The Methodist Hymnal* in 1905, three melodies that had been submitted accompanied it, but the one composed by Karl Pomeroy Harrington has proved to be the favorite. Born in Somersworth, New Hampshire, June 13, 1861, he wrote the music to this carol while at his summer home. Later he expressed his joy in it as it was related to a unique experience — " It was a pleasure when I was taking a trip around the world, to hear the carol sung by school children in Japan, Korea, China, and India." He was Professor of Latin at the University of North Carolina, taught at the University of Maine, but returned to Wesleyan University, Middletown, Connecticut, his alma mater, in 1905, where he continued to teach until his retirement in 1929.

49 *Thou Didst Leave Thy Throne*

Emily E. S. Elliott, 1864   Timothy R. Matthews, 1876

Thou didst leave Thy throne and Thy kingly crown
  When Thou camest to earth for me;
But in Bethlehem's home there was found no room
  For Thy holy nativity.
  O come to my heart, Lord Jesus,
  There is room in my heart for Thee.

Heaven's arches rang when the angels sang,
  Proclaiming Thy royal degree;
But in lowly birth didst Thou come to earth,
  And in great humility.

The foxes found rest, and the birds their nest
  In the shade of the forest tree;
But Thy couch was the sod, O Thou Son of God,
  In the deserts of Galilee.

Thou camest, O Lord, with the living Word
  That should set Thy people free;
But with mocking scorn and with crown of thorn,
  They bore Thee to Calvary.

When the heavens shall ring and the angels sing
  At Thy coming to victory,
Let Thy voice call me home, saying, " Yet there is room,
  There is room at My side for thee! "
  And my heart shall rejoice, Lord Jesus,
  When Thou comest and callest for me.

Emily Elizabeth Steele Elliott (1836–1897) was a clergyman's daughter deeply interested in philanthropy and in Evangelical Sunday school work. Her father, Edward B. Elliott, her uncle, Henry V. Elliott, and her aunt, Charlotte Elliott, were gifted authors, the latter leaving us the familiar hymn "Just as I Am, Without One Plea."

Besides contributing to various collections, she published two volumes of *Hymns and Poems* from 1873 to 1880, a total of one hundred and forty-one hymns. Forty-eight of her second volume were published separately as *Under the Pillow,* a large inexpensive volume for hospitals, infirmaries, and the sick generally.

The hymn " Thou Didst Leave Thy Throne " was privately printed for the choir and school of St. Mark's Church, Brighton, England, served by her father. The text for the hymn is Luke 2:7, " There was no room for them in the inn," and John 1:11, " He came unto his own, and his own received him not."

While the concepts are theological and the hymn is worth studying with Phil. 2:5-11; I Peter 3:22; and Heb. 1:2-8 as a basis, the language is descriptive, using the imagery of the Bible. For this reason the hymn is varyingly classified as for children, Advent, Nativity, evangelism, even as general.

A plan of a series of contrasts can be seen running through the stanzas:

Stanza one — " Throne and crown " versus " no room."

Stanza two — Though of " royal degree " yet " great humility."

Stanza three — Foxes and birds have homes but the Son finds himself in a desert.

Stanza four — Though offering redemption, He is borne to Calvary.

Stanza five — The heavens proclaim victory and room is found on earth for him, and in heaven for me.

W. B. Allen, a poet, has beautifully described for us what " room for the Christ-child " can mean:

> The blasts of winter are fierce and cold,
> The snow lies deep over hill and wold,
> But a star shines bright through the deepening gloom;
> Room for the Christ-child, room.

Where man's distrust and his greed for gain
Have frozen the floods of tender rain,
Till never a flower of hope can bloom:
Room for the Christ-child, room.

In homes that deepest griefs have borne,
'Mid silent forms of those that mourn,
In the shadows that gather around the tomb;
Room for the Christ-child, room.

Where nations are warring, life for life,
And a cry rings out from the fearful strife
As a dying people sinks to its doom;
Room for the Christ-child, room.

Room for the shepherds of Bethlehem,
Room for the angels who sang to them,
Room for the light in the wintry gloom;
Room for the Christ-child, room.

The stanzas can be used very effectively when sung as a solo followed by the refrain as a soft prayer response by the choir or the congregation.

The hymn tune was composed in 1876 by Rev. Timothy Richard Matthews (1826–1910). He called it "Margaret," but it is more commonly known as "Elliott," after the author of the verses. Mr. Matthews was an English clergyman and musician serving at St. Mary's, Nottingham, for six years and at North Coates, Lincolnshire, for forty-eight years. He composed over one hundred hymn tunes and edited several hymnbooks.

Sir John Bowring, 1825   Lowell Mason, 1792–1872

Watchman, tell us of the night,
    What its signs of promise are:
Traveler, o'er yon mountain's height,
    See that glory-beaming star!
Watchman, doth its beauteous ray
    Aught of joy or hope foretell?
Traveler, yes, it brings the day,
    Promised day of Israel.

Watchman, tell us of the night;
    Higher yet that star ascends;
Traveler, blessedness and light,
    Peace and truth, its course portends.
Watchman, will its beams alone
    Gild the spot that gave them birth?
Traveler, ages are its own,
    See, it bursts o'er all the earth!

Watchman, tell us of the night,
    For the morning seems to dawn:
Traveler, darkness takes its flight;
    Doubt and terror are withdrawn.
Watchman, let thy wanderings cease;
    Hie thee to thy quiet home.
Traveler, lo, the Prince of Peace,
    Lo, the Son of God is come!

We have before us a truly unique author as also a unique
song. Sir John Bowring was born at Exeter, England, in
1792. Though a member of the Unitarian Church, his evangelical
faith is indicated by the words of one of his hymns, "In the Cross of
Christ I Glory," being engraved on his tombstone. Though he left

school at fourteen, at the age of sixteen he had acquired five languages, and late in life is said to have known two hundred and spoken one hundred.

As the son of a manufacturer of woolen goods he spent his early years traveling for his father's business. He was elected to the British Parliament and later became the British consul at Canton and the governor of Hong Kong. He published a book of hymns in 1825 to strengthen the religious faith of others who under disheartening circumstances might come to read them. Sir John Bowring is reported to have told Dr. A. P. Hopper in China that the first time he heard this hymn used was in 1834 or 1835 when he attended a prayer meeting of American missionaries in Asiatic Turkey.

The hymn consists of a dialogue between a watchman and a traveler and repeats the question of Isa. 21:11, 12: " Watchman, what of the night? Watchman, what of the night? " This is a rather obscure passage in all the older Bible translations. It is considerably clearer in the Revised Standard Version:

One is calling to me from Seir [Edom, south of the Dead Sea],
   " Watchman, what of the night?
   Watchman, what of the night? "
The watchman says:
" Morning comes, and also the night.
   If you will inquire, inquire;
   come back again."

Seir is evidently in trouble (night) and is looking for relief (morning). He is calling Judah to see if relief is in sight. Judah answers, " Yes and no." That is, the future will bring both good and bad, for you and for me. " Inquire again."

John Bowring's hymn is a moving dramatization of the bright side of this oracle. It interprets the " morning " in a Messianic sense. The new day is the coming of Christ, the " Sun of Righteousness " who shall bless the earth with peace and truth.

The three stanzas show a steady progression toward the dawn of a more perfect day:

Stanza one refers the traveler to the star coming over the mountain.

Stanza two sees the star ascending higher and the light spreading over the earth.

Stanza three reports the dawning of the morning and the coming of the Prince of Peace.

It is clear that the song is largely a result of the author's vivid imagination rather than a delineation of the Nativity story. In fact, Bowring may have had not only the coming of Christ in mind as realized in Bethlehem, but he may have sought to speak to the social conditions of his time as also to the missionary movement of his day.

Our author lived in the post-Napoleonic period when postwar misery was common. Added to that was the dislocation caused by the Industrial Revolution. Trade unions were made legal only in the very year this hymn was written. Slavery was abolished in all British domains in 1833.

Not only during Advent and Christmas but for emphasizing missions does this song have a message. It frequently is placed in hymnals right alongside of " Jesus Shall Reign Where'er the Sun " and " From Greenland's Icy Mountains." The symbolism of " Higher yet that star ascends," " The morning seems to dawn," " See, it bursts o'er all the earth " may have been intended to express the increasing concern of those who had the gospel for those who were without it. In any case, they have come to do so in an inspiring manner.

The music is by Lowell Mason, born January 8, 1792, at Medfield, Massachusetts, where at sixteen years of age he was a choir leader and teacher of singing classes. He reported that he spent twenty years of his life at nothing save playing on all available instruments. At twenty-three he took a position in a bank in Savannah, Georgia. He studied harmony with a Mr. F. L. Abel, who assisted him in 1818 in compiling a book of choral music which ultimately ran through seventeen editions and more than fifty thousand copies.

Later he served as choir leader of three of Boston's choirs, but resigned in order to devote his energies toward introducing music as a regular subject into the public schools. Through his musical conventions, the publication of much material for them as well as for public and Sunday school, Lowell Mason probably contributed more to music in America than any other individual.

His musical tunes are excellent and have gained a strong foothold in English and European books.

The tune for the song under discussion lends itself excellently to antiphonal use. The composer had in mind a duet for soprano and tenor, with the congregation repeating the reply to the questions.

It is interesting to note also the striking fact that the author of the hymn and the composer of the tune were contemporaries in an unusual degree, both having been born in 1792 and both having died in 1872.

---

51 We Three Kings of Orient Are

John Henry Hopkins, Jr., 1857   John Henry Hopkins, Jr., 1857

KINGS:
    We three kings of Orient are,
    Bearing gifts we traverse afar
      Field and fountain, moor and mountain,
    Following yonder star.
        O star of wonder, star of night,
        Star with royal beauty bright,
          Westward leading, still proceeding,
        Guide us to the perfect light.

MELCHIOR:
    Born a babe on Bethlehem's plain,
    Gold I bring to crown Him again;
      King forever, ceasing never
    Over us all to reign.

CASPAR:
    Frankincense to offer have I;
    Incense owns a Deity nigh,
      Prayer and praising all men raising,
    Worship Him, God on high.

BALTHASAR: Myrrh is mine; its bitter perfume
              Breathes a life of gathering gloom;
                  Sorrowing, sighing, bleeding, dying,
              Sealed in the stone-cold tomb.

ALL: Glorious now behold Him arise,
              King and God and Sacrifice;
                  Heaven sings " Hallelujah! "
              " Hallelujah! " earth replies.

Both text and tune of this song, " one of the most successful modern examples," according to *The Oxford Book of Carols,* a standard authority in the field, were written by John H. Hopkins, Jr. (1820–1891). He was born in Pittsburgh and received his higher education at the University of Vermont, in which state his father was bishop in the Episcopal Church.

He produced this beloved carol while rector of Christ Church, Williamsport, Pennsylvania, in 1857. Of the collection of his verses entitled *Poems by the Wayside Written During More than Forty Years,* published in 1883, this carol is his best. In fact, it has the unique characteristic that may class it as a masterpiece of its sort, in that the tune " Kings of Orient " has so delicately achieved the folk song manner that Hopkins has quite often been erroneously referred to as the arranger instead of the composer.

Because the content reflects so much that is traditional and legendary, some few have disregarded the song and failed to appreciate its unique beauty and appeal.

It is one of the few songs that are based on the story of the Wise Men (Matt. 2:1-12), as compared with the many based on the story of the shepherds (Luke, ch. 2). The tradition that there were three Wise Men (the number is not mentioned in Scripture) no doubt arose through the unjustified conclusion that three kinds of gifts were brought by three men. The names Melchior, Caspar, and Balthasar are, of course, legendary. The gifts indicate a helpful symbolism: gold stands for Christ's royalty; frankincense indicates his divinity; and myrrh refers prophetically to his suffering.

116

According to legend, the three kings, the Wise Men, arrived on the twelfth night after Jesus' birth to present their gifts. Hence the custom, in some countries, of exchanging gifts on Twelfth-night.

The stanzas lend themselves admirably for dramatic presentation and are so used very frequently. All three monarchs join in the first stanza and tell of their following the star. Then, in turn, each one sings alone — Melchior, Caspar, and Balthasar — telling of his special gift to the Child and what the gift symbolizes. Finally the three unite in the fifth stanza.

However prominent the legendary element may be, there is nowhere else any more impressive description of the star of Bethlehem:

> O star of wonder, star of night,
> Star with royal beauty bright,
>> Westward leading, still proceeding,
> Guide us to the perfect light.

---

52 We Would See Jesus; Lo! His Star Is Shining

J. Edgar Park, 1913   Herbert B. Turner, 1905

> We would see Jesus; lo! His star is shining
>> Above the stable while the angels sing;
> There in a manger on the hay reclining,
>> Haste, let us lay our gifts before the King.

> We would see Jesus, Mary's Son most holy,
>> Light of the village life from day to day,
> Shining revealed through every task most lowly,
>> The Christ of God, the Life, the Truth, the Way.

> We would see Jesus on the mountain teaching,
>> With all the listening people gathered round;
> While birds and flowers and sky above are preaching
>> The blessedness which simple trust has found.

We would see Jesus; in the early morning
　　Still as of old He calleth, " Follow Me ";
Let us arise, all meaner service scorning;
　　Lord, we are Thine, we give ourselves to Thee.

(Words from *New Worship and Song*. Copyright, The Pilgrim Press. Used by permission. Music also available in the Evangelical and Methodist hymnals.)

It is doubly pleasant when we have undisputed facts before us concerning both the words and the music of a song. That is the case with this comparatively recent hymn.

Since original sources are seldom available, we make use now of the opportunity to quote from two private letters of the author, Dr. J. Edgar Park, late president of Wheaton College, Norton, Massachusetts, with the kind permission of his widow, Mrs. J. Edgar Park. In one of them he indicates the occasion for writing the song.

" It was written for a hymnal published by The Pilgrim Press of Boston [*New Worship and Song*] and the lady in charge returned it, I remember, thinking some of the lines could be improved. The line ' Light of the village life from day to day ' came as the result of revision. . . . The tune ' Cushman,' to which it is set in the hymnal in which it was first published, was in my mind as I wrote it. The hymn is a ' Song of Youth.' "

In a second letter, he goes into greater detail, as follows:

" A lady connected with a new hymnbook being issued by The Pilgrim Press suggested to me that there were great possibilities in the motive ' We would see Jesus ' for a hymn. There was an existing hymn with this first line, but the note struck by it was a minor one, more suited for old age and the disillusioned outlook of elderly people seeking escape and comfort from religion. I thought that the line could be used for a hymn for youth and promise and sunshine equally well. The tune was written for it and, if I remember right, was in my hands as I began to think over the theme. I had just published two studies of the Sermon on the Mount, and the vision of the youthful Teacher, of the divine Boy, of the Leader of strength and greatness was in my mind. The hymn was born out of a first line, a tune, and an inner glimpse of the Young Man of Nazareth living and moving among us. The line 'Light of the village life from day to day' was not in the hymn in its first version. The lady mentioned above wrote me suggesting that there was one weak line for which after hours of meditation I substituted this line as it now stands."

John Edgar Park was born at Belfast, Ireland, the son, grandson, great-grandson, and father of ministers of the gospel. After studying at New College, Edinburgh; the Presbyterian Theological Seminary at Belfast; and at the Royal University, Dublin, he came to this country in 1900, entered Princeton Theological Seminary, and was ordained to the Presbyterian ministry in 1903. After serving as pastor of the West Parish Church, Andover, and of the Second Congregational Church, West Newton, Massachusetts, he was called to the presidency of Wheaton College, Norton, Massachusetts, in 1906. Here he rendered distinguished service as an educator and also found time to write a half dozen books, and in addition to deliver the Beecher Lectures at Yale in 1935.

Since too often a hymn is classified completely according to the content of its first stanza only, it is used only in a certain season — Christmas in this case. The complete hymn is, however, a beautiful summary of the entire life of our Lord and invites, toward the end, a wholehearted consecration of life and service to him. Its objective historical and practical character commends it for repeated use, not only at Christmas but throughout the year.

The tune " Cushman " was originally written for the hymn upon which this one is based as to form, namely, " We Would See Jesus; for the Shadows Lengthen." It was written by Herbert B. Turner while he was editing *Hymns and Tunes for Schools* at Hampton Normal and Agricultural Institute at Hampton, Virginia. The author relates, " I got the tune singing in my head so that I could go nowhere without it, and then gradually one verse after another began singing itself to the tune." It was first published in this collection in 1907 and six years later in a book, *New Worship and Song*.

The composer, born in Brooklyn, July 17, 1852, preached in a small parish church in Brooklyn before going to Hampton Institute, where he served as chaplain until his retirement in 1925. He helped to edit three books of hymns and tunes. He died at Washington, Connecticut, May 1, 1927.

---

53 *What Child Is This?*

Wm. C. Dix, 1837–1898

Old English Melody
" My Lady Greensleeves "
Arr. by Sir John Stainer

What Child is this, who, laid to rest,
  On Mary's lap is sleeping?
Whom angels greet with anthems sweet,
  While shepherds watch are keeping?
This, this is Christ the King,
Whom shepherds guard and angels sing:
Haste, haste to bring Him laud,
The Babe, the Son of Mary!

Why lies He in such mean estate,
  Where ox and ass are feeding?
Good Christian, fear: for sinners here
  The silent Word is pleading.
Nails, spear, shall pierce Him through,
The cross be borne, for me for you:
Hail, hail, the Word made flesh,
The Babe, the Son of Mary!

So bring Him incense, gold, and myrrh,
  Come, peasant, king, to own Him;
The King of Kings salvation brings,
  Let loving hearts enthrone Him.

Raise, raise the song on high,
The Virgin sings her lullaby:
Joy, joy, for Christ is born,
The Babe, the Son of Mary!

(Music available in *Carols, Customs and Costumes Around the World*. The Old Orchard Publishers, Webster Groves, Mo.)

William Chatterton Dix (1837–1898), an insurance man with a turn for writing hymns (see "As with Gladness Men of Old "), though manager of a marine insurance company in Glasgow, continued his literary interest. He wrote the *Life of Chatterton, the Poet; Pen Pictures of Popular English Classics,* and several volumes of devotional poetry.

The appealing carol before us was written by him after he had been ill in bed on Epiphany Day and, after reading the Gospel for the day, he finished the carol that same evening. It became very popular and is found in most English hymnals.

The reference to the manger bed in stanza two is, of course, inaccurate since the star that guided the Wise Men stood over the house where the child was (Matt. 2:9-11).

The tune is a clear illustration of a folk tune being adapted to a new set of verses. The adaptation is indicated in the name commonly given to the tune " My Lady Greensleeves," a song which was popular during the reign of Queen Elizabeth and was referred to by Shakespeare as being one of the most popular of his day. These are the authentic words of this charming English love song:

Alas, my love, you do me wrong
To cast me off discourteously,
For I have lovèd you so long
Delighting in your company.
Greensleeves was all my joy,
Greensleeves was my delight,
Greensleeves was my heart of gold,
And all for my Lady Greensleeves.

The "Old English Air" or "My Lady Greensleeves" as it has come to be known, was arranged by Sir John Stainer into the form that we know it with "What Child Is This?"

Sir John Stainer (1840–1901) was a prolific composer of church music and a distinguished organist. He served as organist at the University of Oxford and later at St. Paul's Cathedral. In America he is perhaps best known for his great cantata *The Crucifixion,* along with the arrangement of the melody for this carol. The latter is a joyous tune which may be sung as a solo, or with the sopranos singing the words of the stanzas while the other voices hum the accompaniments, climaxing in all parts singing the refrain in harmony or in unison.

54   *While Shepherds Watched Their Flocks*

Nahum Tate, 1703   George Frederick Handel, 1728

While shepherds watched their flocks by night,
 All seated on the ground,
The angel of the Lord came down,
 And glory shone around,
 And glory shone around.

" Fear not," he said — for mighty dread
 Had seized their troubled mind —
" Glad tidings of great joy I bring
 To you and all mankind,
 To you and all mankind.

" To you in David's town this day
 Is born of David's line,
The Saviour, who is Christ, the Lord,
 And this shall be the sign:
 And this shall be the sign:

"The heavenly Babe you there shall find
　　To human view displayed,
All meanly wrapped in swathing bands,
　　And in a manger laid,
　　And in a manger laid."

Thus spake the seraph, and forthwith
　　Appeared a shining throng
Of angels praising God, who thus
　　Addressed their joyful song:
　　Addressed their joyful song:

"All glory be to God on high,
　　And to the earth be peace:
Good will henceforth, from heaven to men,
　　Begin and never cease,
　　Begin and never cease!"

Not only is "While Shepherds Watched Their Flocks" sung wherever the English language is spoken, but it has been translated into Latin (four versions) and into nearly all the living languages today.

To appreciate this song we must know the author and remember that he lived in the days of a psalm-singing Church. It came into being as a part of the efforts of English poets to provide a Christian hymnody for the Church, distinct from the Psalms of the Old Testament. That may partly explain why it is more a paraphrase of Scripture, specifically of Luke 2:9-11, than an original composition.

The author, Nahum Tate (1652–1715), jointly with Nicholas Brady, published in 1696 *A New Version of the Psalms of David, Fitted to the Tunes Used in Churches,* followed in 1700 by a *Supplement to the New Version* containing sixteen hymns, among them "While Shepherds Watched Their Flocks." All have been forgotten except this one.

One of the complaints against the *New Version* was that it was too "showy" and too "poetical." It was said, "David speaks so plain that we cannot mistake his meaning, but as for Mr. Tate and Mr. Brady, they have taken away our Lord and we know not where they have laid him!"

Thomas Jefferson, on the other hand, recommended the reading of Tate and Brady's version of the Fifteenth Psalm, "knowing nothing more moral, more sublime and more worthy of your perusing."

It is interesting to observe minor modifications in modern versions by comparing them with an early edition:

Stanza one — While humble shepherds watched their flocks
In Bethlehem's plains by night,
An angel sent from heaven appeared
And filled the plains with light.

Stanza six — Good will is shown by heaven to men,
And never more shall cease.

So also, in 1745, the first stanza was revised for the Scottish *Translation and Paraphrases,* and the alteration is used to this day in the hymnbooks of Scotland, essentially as above. The Scottish revisers also changed Tate's "mighty dread" in the first line of the second stanza to "sudden dread."

The verses were written for the tune "Winchester Old," an old English hymn tune first published by Thomas Este in 1592 in his *Psalter.* More frequently the words are sung to a carol tune of Richard Storr Willis which we have come to associate with "It Came Upon the Midnight Clear."

Most frequently the carol is now sung to "Christmas," an arrangement from a soprano aria in Act II of Handel's opera *Siroe* (1728). It is joyous, uplifting, and well suited to the words that it carries.

George Frederick Handel, though born at Halle, Prussia, in 1685, lived in England fifty years and became a naturalized citizen. As the founder of the traditional English oratorio, he was greatly beloved by the English people. Born in the same year as Johann Sebastian Bach, he outlived the latter by nine years. Both men were deeply religious and have left their impress upon religious music of all types.

Historians of music rightly call the first half of the eighteenth century the age of Bach and Handel.

While Handel wrote only three hymn tunes, there have been many arrangements or adaptations from his numerous works. During Christmas time his most popular composition, *The Messiah,* is widely enjoyed. This oratorio, written in twenty-three days, was sung in London in the presence of the king. When the choir sang " For the Lord God Omnipotent reigneth " in the majestic " Hallelujah Chorus," the king and all the assembly rose (or were lifted) to their feet, thus establishing a custom that continues to this day. This pointedly symbolizes what all the Christmas songs should convey to us, " Rejoice and be glad, lift up your heads — your Saviour has come and He reigns even now! "

National and Racial Grouping

For use in connection with program planning, the songs in this book have been classified below into national and racial groups. In a majority of cases, the classification is based on the words of the song, but wherever the melody or the story of its origin has been popularly associated with the song, that factor has determined the grouping.